# DEALING WITH GRIEF AND LOSS

P9-CRK-595

## HOPE IN THE MIDST OF PAIN

**SERENDIPITY EXECUTIVE EDITORS:**
Lyman Coleman and Marty Scales

**SUPPORT SERIES EDITOR:**
Richard Peace

**PRINCIPLE AUTHORS:**
William Cutler
Richard Peace

**CONTRIBUTING WRITER:**
David Terry

**COVER LAYOUT:**
Steve Eames

**CARTOONIST:**
Robert Shull

**LAYOUT PRODUCTION TEAM:**
John Winson
Doug LaBudde
Patricia Picardi

# SERENDIPITY SUPPORT GROUP SERIES

ADDITIONAL BOOKS AVAILABLE
IN THE **SERENDIPITY SUPPORT GROUP SERIES**:


**BLENDED FAMILIES:** Yours, Mine, Ours

**MIDLIFE:** The Crisis That Brings Renewal

**PARENTING ADOLESCENTS:** Easing the Way to Adulthood

**NEWLY MARRIED:** How to Have a Great First Year


OTHER BOOKS TO FOLLOW

94 95 96 / CHG / 10 9 8 7 6 5 4 3 2

# Dealing With Grief and Loss
## Hope in the Midst of Pain

**PURPOSE** 

1. **What is this course all about?** Becoming a support group while discussing a Biblical perspective on the feelings experienced during times of grief and loss.

**AUDIENCE**

2. **Who is this course designed for?** Anyone who is facing a situation of loss who would like to have the support of others.

**NEW PEOPLE**

3. **Is this only for church people?** Absolutely not—this group is for everyone. While this series is oriented around a Christian perspective, no church commitment or background is assumed or necessary.

**STUDY**

4. **What are we going to study?** Based on the research done by Dr. Elizabeth Kübler-Ross, this study deals with the feelings common to people who have experienced loss. Such feelings may come about as a result of a severe health problem, a disability, a divorce, being fired or laid off, the death of a loved one, or some other experience that radically alters our life and leaves us wondering what life is all about.

**DURATION**

5. **How long will the course last?** There is enough material for fourteen small group sessions. Each chapter has two sessions in it.

**THE TWO SESSIONS**

6. **How do the two sessions differ?** The first session in each chapter is entitled: *Examining the Issue*. It focuses on crucial concepts necessary to understand the process of grief and loss. The second session is entitled: *Bible Study*. It focuses on various passages from Scripture related to the aspect of grief and loss that is under consideration.

**7 WEEK OPTION**

7. **What if we don't have 14 weeks?** You can do the course in as little as seven weeks. In that case, do only one of the two sessions in each chapter. Assign the other for homework.

**LENGTH OF SESSIONS**

8. **How long is each small group session?** Sixty minutes. Suggested times for each part of the session are given in the book.

| | |
|---|---|
| **STICKING TO THE TIME** | 9. **What if we can't complete an exercise in the allotted time?** The times that are given are just suggestions. However, if you go overtime in one exercise, you will have less time for the other exercises. In fact, you may not be able to use all the questions in each exercise. Don't worry about this. Just pick and choose the questions that fit the needs and interests of the group. |
| **90 MINUTE OPTION** | 10. **What if we can't finish all the exercises in 60 minutes?** Some groups find that they get into such good discussions that sixty minutes is not enough time, even when they pick and choose questions. In this case, renegotiate with your small group for an extra 30 minutes. Whatever you decide, be sure to end the session at the agreed time. |
| **AGENDA** | 11. **What is the purpose of each of the four parts of the small group interaction?** The *Open* exercise gives group members the chance to tell their stories to one another. It helps them get to know one another, it provides the opportunity for people to check in with each other each week, and it provides an easy way to begin thinking about the topic. The *Consider* section provides new input for the group about the topic. The *Discuss* section gets the group talking about the ideas in the *Consider* section. And the *Respond* section provides a chance to apply the ideas to each person's situation. |
| **BIBLE KNOWLEDGE** | 12. **What if I don't know much about the Bible?** That's all right. Reference notes on the Bible passages discussed will fill in needed background information. |
| **REFERENCE NOTES** | 13. **What is the purpose of the Reference Notes?** To help you understand the context of the Bible passage, and any difficult words that need to be defined. |
| **LEADERSHIP** | 14. **Who leads the meetings?** Anyone may guide these discussions. The leader is not a teacher or a counselor, but a facilitator to get the group started and keep it on track. One person can lead all the time, or you can rotate leadership among the members. |
| **WHAT THE GROUP IS** | 15. **What is at the heart of this group?** This is a support group. This is a group in which we can share our grief experiences. This is a group where we can learn together, pray together, laugh together, and, if necessary, cry together. This is a group that will attempt to help us get through our pain and loss. |
| **WHAT THE GROUP IS NOT** | 16. **What will not take place in this group?** This is not a therapy group. This is not a lecture by an expert. This is not a gripe group. This is not group counseling. |

**RESOURCES**

17. **Where can I find more material on this subject?** At the end of the book you will find a bibliography of helpful books and some suggestions about further Bible studies on the topic.

**GROUP COVENANT**

18. **What are the ground rules for the group?**

☐ **Priority**: While you are in the course, you give the group meetings priority.

☐ **Participation**: Generally the pattern is that everyone participates and no one dominates. However, since grief work seems to come in spurts, there will be times when a particular person needs to be able to dominate the meeting for a while.

☐ **Respect**: Everyone is given the right to their own opinion and "dumb questions" are encouraged and respected. No one judges, no one criticizes.

☐ **Openness**: The aim of the small group is to support one another in the process of grief. This can only happen if each person is willing to be candid about his or her life situation.

☐ **Confidentiality**: Anything that is said in the meeting is never repeated outside the meeting.

☐ **Support**: Permission is given to call upon each other in time of need.

**CONTINUING**

19. **What happens to the group after finishing the course?** The group is free to disband or continue to another course. In Chapter 7 you will find various suggestions for continuing on as a group. Call Toll Free 800-525-9563 for suggestions about other courses and to receive a free Serendipity Resource Catalog.

# On Dealing with Grief and Loss:
## Some Comments on the Way This Course Is Structured

Grief and loss come in many forms. In fact, each person's experience is unique. Because this is so, it is not possible to prepare a study guide that will take into account the entire range of grief experiences. Yet it is also true that the feelings we experience during our grief are common to all of us. These shared feelings are the foundation on which we can become a support group for one another.

**PURPOSE OF THE GROUP**

The purpose of this group is to support one another during the process of grieving. It is not to "get through" all the material in this book. The material is secondary. Its purpose is to create the climate of openness and understanding that will bring about new insight and facilitate mutual sharing and caring. As such, it is useful for you to know the intent of each section of the book.

**EXAMINING THE ISSUE**

This sections seeks to provide insight into the nature of the grieving process. To know that what we are experiencing—the pain, the numbness, the confusion, the raging emotions, the lack of emotion—is similar to what others have experienced, is a comfort. To have some handles on the process itself is useful (though more so to some than others).

**THE SHARING EXERCISES**

The small group exercises move to the heart of why the group was formed. These exercises focus and guide the group conversation. They facilitate the processing of what is going on inside each person. The *Open* sections, in particular, aim at providing a way to get people to talk about themselves and their lives. They provide a way for each person to declare: "This is who I am in my uniqueness, and this is what I am going through right now." The *Open* exercises are of two kinds. Those that precede the Examine the Issue sections are reminiscent in nature. They often look back into childhood in order to find experiences in which similar feelings were elictied to what people are experiencing now. The *Open* exercises that come before the Bible Study give people an opportunity to talk at more length about their losses. These times of focused sharing may turn out for many to be the richest times (although not necessarily the easiest).

**EXPRESSING GRIEF**

People express grief in different ways. Some of us share our concerns easily and enjoy talking things out. Others of us take time to gain the confidence to share, or to collect our thoughts in an articulate fashion. In any event, it is essential that the group develop the ability to listen carefully. It does not matter if a person speaks first or last, a lot or a little. What is important is that we afford each other the opportunity to share in our own ways, and that we pay close attention to what each person shares. Good listening will make us sensitive to each other's pain and stimulate our own thoughts concerning our particular grief.

**BIBLE STUDY** The Bible studies have their own role to play in the small group experience. It is their purpose to point people beyond themselves to God. They seek to remind the group of the reality and presence of God. True, it is the absence of God that is sometimes the overwhelming feeling one has in the face of tragedy. "Where is God?" "Why did God let this happen?" "Why don't I sense God's presence?" people ask. But there is a deeper truth that underlies such feelings: the truth that God is, that God does care, that God loves us, and that God forever demonstrated all these facts by sending his Son to die for us (to show us that love is stronger than death and that it will win out in the end). Death is not the last word—resurrection is. We need to know this even when we can't feel it. We need to understand that in Christ's death, our suffering is comprehended and borne by God. In his resurrection we find our eternal hope: a victory over all grief and loss. In our communion with Christ, we can affirm the goodness of God, who works good in the midst of the sorrows of human existence.

**THE BOOK OF JOB** We will be focusing on the Book of Job in the Bible studies. Job, with its gritty reality, raw emotion, and seemingly senseless suffering, touches a deep place in us. We can relate to what Job is saying and feeling, and why. In Job, we come upon the reality of God in the midst of all the pain and suffering. We find a person who knows the living Redeemer and believes in a resurrection in the midst of grief. It is the reality of Job's experience of suffering that speaks to us, and his relationship with God that inspires our faith. Certainly countless men and women down through the ages have touched the power of God through the Book of Job.

**EXPECTATIONS** What can we legitimately hope will happen to us by being part of a group like this? This is hard to answer, since people will have such different needs. Certainly the chance to talk openly about their loss in the context of a caring group will be of value to everyone, no matter at what stage of grief they find themselves. But still, it needs to be recognized that grief is a long process. It will not be over in the fourteen weeks of this group. Furthermore, there will be some people who are having a particularly hard time that will need professional help, or the more intense step-by-step program outlined in the Cherry and James book: *The Grief Recovery Handbook*. In any case, after fourteen weeks you will have a group of friends with whom you can continue to be open about your grief, and that alone will be a great blessing.

Blessings on you as you begin this support group.

# When It All Collapses

The aims of the two sessions in this chaper are:

- To begin to get to know each other, and to identify the experience of loss that we will each focus on in these small group meetings.
- To become acquainted with the various feelings and problems which people experience during times of grief and loss.
- To begin an exploration of the Book of Job and its account of someone struggling to come to terms with suffering in his life.

| 1 | Examining the Issue | 60 Minutes |
|---|---|---|

**OPEN**

**LEADER:**
Go around the group and, beginning with yourself, let each person respond *briefly* to the first question. Do the same for each question until time runs out for this section.

Introductions (15 minutes).

1. Take one minute to share a little bit about who you are. Talk about where you live and work, your family, how long you have lived in the community, etc.

2. What are one or two things you really enjoy doing?

3. How did you hear about this group?

**CONSIDER**

**Consider the following information about the feelings people experience when they are grieving (5 minutes).**

**LEADER:**
Present this material while the group follows along in the text.

Grief marks us as human.

Regardless of one's race, social class, economic status, religion, or gender, all people will experience grief. On the issue of suffering, no one stands apart. Perhaps this is why the author of the Epistle to the Hebrews wrote that Jesus (who suffered rejection, temptation, pain, and death) is "of the same family" as you and I (He 2:10-11). While grief typically causes a person to feel isolated and terribly alone, it actually may be the one experience that unites a person with every other person on this planet.

Hardship comes in various guises. And it seldom give us time to prepare for it:

- A man comes home from work one day to find a note from his wife saying that she has left him.

9

- A routine visit to the doctor leads to the discovery of cancer.
- The pink slip nestled in a single mother's pay envelope informs her that she is one of those who is to be laid off work.
- Icy roads result in yet another traffic fatality, but this time it is a loved one who is killed.
- A summer swim results in a broken neck from a careless dive.
- The person you were planning to marry decides to end the relationship.

Our world is shattered by events that force us to face the fact that all too often life is harsh, unstable, and capricious. There is no predictability, no clear-cut cause-and-effect relationship, no control. Suddenly, life feels like a car that has hit a hidden patch of ice. The steering wheel is wrenched from our hands and spins wildly in front of us, mocking our attempts to grab onto it. We feel trapped by forces too big for us. Panic and fear grab us by the throat and won't let go.

Any situation that leads to a major loss—be it a divorce, a death, a severe injury, a natural disaster, the loss of a job— produces these feelings. Counselors, influenced by the pioneering work of Dr. Elizabeth Kübler-Ross, have found that after such a loss, people typically go through an unfolding series of emotional responses. *Grief, they find, is a process, not a singular event.*

Understanding the process of grief, of course, is not the same as going through it. Nor will understanding it mean that a grieving person can "get it over with" faster. When suffering comes our way, grief will affect us whether we understand its dynamics or not. However, understanding the grief process can help us at such times to recall that we are not alone; others have felt what we are feeling. Others have grieved as we grieve and have survived. We also understand that grief is normal, not abnormal; grief marks us as human. Understanding the grief process can also help us be better friends to those who are experiencing sorrow. It can help us accept where they actually are in their feelings, and not pressure them to be somewhere else in the process. It can help us not to be surprised by their feelings and actions.

According to Dr. Kübler-Ross, the grief process has five stages:

• *Denial*: The "this cannot be happening to me" feeling. This is when a person simply cannot face the facts of what is actually happening.

• *Anger*: The sense of disbelief turns toward blaming oneself or others. Anger comes unexpectedly and is hard to control.

• *Bargaining*: Often a person will think "If only..." thoughts: "If only she would move back in, I'd make it up to her. This time I'll do the right thing." A superficial sense of hope may develop.

• *Depression*: This is the recognition that real loss has occurred and nothing can be done about it. The feeling of hopelessness and of powerlessness to change anything can be overwhelming.

• *Acceptance*: This involves submission to the new reality. It is a state of emotional balance reached after the tumult of a major change. A person is able to deal realistically with his or her new status in life.

The various feelings associated with grief occur at different times for different people, and they last longer for some people than for others. Furthermore, though we may talk about this process in terms of stages, in actuality the stages often merge together. A person may experience two or three of these feelings at the same time. Or he or she may experience one dominant emotion on many levels. For example, a husband may be angry toward the person who drove the car that killed his wife; angry that his wife died and left him alone; angry when he cannot balance his checking account (since his wife always handled that responsibility). He may experience anger each time he comes to grips with new implications of his loss. There is no clear-cut, "normal" time frame that determines how a person will experience all the stages of grief.

Typically, grief lasts from 18 months to 2 years. But don't try to fit your experience into some sort of standard timetable. And don't try to program your grief according to some sort of hard and fast "normal" pattern. But do deal with your grief. Your aim is recovery. Recovery is, simply, feeling better. It is being able to recall the loved one without getting wrought up inside. It is recalling the rich memories of the old neighborhood while enjoying your new home. This doesn't happen automatically (you have to work at recovery); time doesn't automatically heal the loss (some people grieve for decades because they have not been able to address their feelings properly). But it can happen as we work openly and directly with our grief, with the help of others. None of us can manage grief on our own, nor were we meant to.

Grief, as it turns out, is not our enemy. Grief is not a mark of weakness, nor a sign of no faith. Grief is normal and necessary. To be sure, grief is hard. Grief takes time. But grief is the way we work through loss. We need to give ourselves (and others) permission to grieve. Grief is nature's way to heal a broken heart.[1]

DISCUSS

**Discuss with the group your response to the following questions (15 minutes).**

1. What motivated you to become a part of this group? Check the box that most nearly describes your reason. Briefly explain your choice to the group. (At various places in each session, you will have the opportunity to share different aspects of your story.)
   - ❏ I am struggling at the moment with a loss.
   - ❏ I am interested in the subject of grief and want to know more about recent insights into the process.
   - ❏ I am concerned about a past loss that has continued to haunt me.
   - ❏ I am involved with a friend who is dealing with a loss.
   - ❏ I want to be able to help others (and myself) through the grief process.
   - ❏ Other:_____.

**LEADER:**
Give the group a few minutes to work on questions 2 and 3. Then allow each person, beginning with yourself, to share *briefly* (one minute) the nature of the loss he or she will focus on over the next weeks together. Go around a second time and let each person express his or her hope.

2. This course is designed for people who are confronting grief in one way or another. For the sharing to be the most meaningful, you will want to focus on a specific experience of grief or loss—past or present. This must be *your* loss, not someone else's. Even if your immediate concern is to help a friend or family member through a tough time, don't focus on their experience. Focus on your experience in the sharing. Take a moment and:
   - ❏ List the losses that you have had in your life.
   - ❏ Identify the one that has the most emotional impact attached to it for you.
   - ❏ Describe this loss to the group.

3. What do you hope to receive from this group?
   - ❏ support
   - ❏ comfort
   - ❏ insight
   - ❏ friendship
   - ❏ someone to listen
   - ❏ other:_____

**LEADER:**
Make sure everyone is clear about the time, place, length, and frequency of meetings.

4. For these sessions to be the most effective, it is necessary to agree on certain ground rules so that everyone is comfortable with the group. Take a few minutes to read the ground rules on page 5. Any questions about what any of these ground rules mean? Any ground rules you think should be added? Any you think should be eliminated?

**RESPOND**

**Split into groups of four. Read the following quotation and then discuss your response to it using the questions that follow (25 minutes).** This selection is taken from *A Grief Observed*, a book written by C.S. Lewis after the death of his wife.

No one ever told me that grief felt so like fear...The same fluttering in the stomach, the same restlessness, the yawning. I keep on swallowing.

At other times it feels like being mildly drunk...There is a sort of invisible blanket between the world and me. I find it hard to take in what anyone says.... Yet I want the others to be about me. I dread the moments when the house is empty. If only they would talk to one another and not to me.

There are moments, most unexpectedly, when something inside me tried to assure me that I don't really mind so much, not so very much, after all. Love is not the whole of a man's life. I was happy before I ever met H. I've plenty of what are called 'resources.' People get over these things.... Then comes a sudden jab of red-hot memory and all this 'common sense' vanishes like an ant in the mouth of a furnace.

On the rebound one passes into tears and pathos. Maudlin tears, I almost prefer the moments of agony.

Meanwhile, where is God?...go to him when your need is desperate, when all other help is vain, and what do you find? A door slammed in your face, and a sound of bolting and double bolting on the inside. After that, silence.[2]

**LEADER:**
Encourage each person to keep a diary or journal of their grief experiences. These can be entirely private, or shared with the group at various times. Such a journal will serve to clarify events and thoughts which are hard to articulate.

1. Have you ever been close to someone going through the grieving process? In what ways was his or her experience similar to what Lewis describes?

2. In your own experiences of grief, in what ways are you experiencing (or have you experienced) emotions similar to what Lewis describes?

3. If you were in Lewis' situation, what would you hope your friends might do for you?

4. Close with a time of silent or conversational prayer, thanking God for bringing you together as a group and asking him to help you grow through this process.

| 2 | **Bible Study** | 60 Minutes |

**OPEN**

**LEADER:**
There are seven opportunities for sharing of this sort. Depending upon how many you have in the group, use this time for one or two stories.

### Sharing our Stories (15 minutes).

Every other week, prior to the Bible Study, we will begin our session by asking one or two members of the group to share in some detail their stories of loss. No response is expected from the group, except to listen attentively. You will have other opportunities to share particular parts of your story as they apply to the topic under consideration. But this exercise will give you the opportunity (if you choose) to go into more detail. Conclude the sharing by spending a few moments in prayer as a group.

**CONSIDER**

**LEADER:**
Present this material while the group follows along in the text.

### Read this introduction before you study the passage.

The story of Job, written by an unknown author in an unknown place, is perhaps the oldest book in the Old Testament. It is a monumental piece of literature, wrestling as it does with the deepest issues of life and refusing to give trivial answers to them.

In the first chapters of the book, the reader is told how, in a matter of days, Job lost his wealth, his children, the respect of his wife, and his health. His suffering goes on, unabated, for an indeterminate length of time. Throughout this ordeal, Job expresses his faith in a living Redeemer. He is joined by three friends who, at first, simply sit with him in silence. After several days, however, when Job still seems to be making no progress with his grief, they begin to offer reasons why he must be going through such awful suffering. Job rejects their arguments as superficial and unfair. "Why" questions are important. We can't avoid asking them, nor should we. The problem is that we can seldom answer such questions. Job himself does not get any answers until the end of his experience when he encounters God, and even then the "answer" he gets is not what he expected.

We pick up the story at a time when, in the midst of his pain, Job questions whether or not God even cares about justice or mercy. This passage reminds us how answers can sound sanctimonious or trite to those who are suffering.

**READ**

**LEADER:**
You might want to read the text aloud. Be sure, however, to allow group members time on their own to reread the text and to go over the reference notes. In particular, the first note is important in order to describe the context of this passage.

Read the passage below. Use the reference notes that follow to enhance your understanding of the text (5 minutes).

*¹Then Job replied:*

*²"Listen carefully to my words;*
*let this be the consolation you give me.*
*³Bear with me while I speak,*
*and after I have spoken, mock on.*

*⁴"Is my complaint directed to man?*
*Why should I not be impatient?*
*⁵Look at me and be astonished;*
*clap your hand over your mouth.*
*⁶When I think about this, I am terrified;*
*trembling seizes my body.*
*⁷Why do the wicked live on,*
*growing old and increasing in power? ...*

*¹³They spend their years in prosperity*
*and go down to the grave in peace.*
*¹⁴Yet they say to God, 'Leave us alone!*
*We have no desire to know your ways.*
*¹⁵Who is the Almighty, that we should serve him?*
*What would we gain by praying to him?'*
*¹⁶But their prosperity is not in their own hands,*
*so I stand aloof from the counsel of the wicked.*

*Job 21:1-7,13-16*

**DISCUSS**

Discuss the passage with your group using the questions which follow (20 minutes).

1. What are the feelings that Job exhibits in this passage? Discuss why he is feeling this way.

| | | |
|---|---|---|
| ☑ pain | ☑ anger | ☐ terror |
| ☐ disillusionment | ☐ fear | ☑ indignation |
| ☐ jealousy | ☐ regret | ☐ abused |
| ☑ frustration | ☐ pity | ☐ impatience |

2. Based on the material in this chapter, which stage of Kübler-Ross' grief process do you think Job is in here? Why?

| | | |
|---|---|---|
| ☐ Denial | ☑ Anger | ☐ Bargaining |
| ☐ Depression | ☐ Acceptance | |

3. How would you respond to Job's comments? What would you say or what would you do?

**RESPOND** | **Wrap up your discussion with these questions (20 minutes).**

1. Which cliche´ best describes how people you know look at life (especially the suffering of others) when things are going well for them?
   - ❏ Everything that goes around, comes around.
   - ❏ God sends rain on the just and the unjust—so both parades get wet.
   - ❏ The righteous shall prosper.
   - ❏ When you get lemons, make lemonade.
   - ❏ Early to bed, early to rise, makes a man healthy, wealthy, and wise.
   - ❏ In every cloud there's a silver lining.
   - ❏ Life is a bowl of cherries...so why complain when you get a pit?
   - ❏ Suffering is only the illusion of a person with inordinate desires.
   - ❏ Everyone gets what they deserve.
   - ❏ What the mind conceives and the will believes, that you can achieve.
   - ❏ Other:_____.

2. What happens to these philosophies when crisis hits?

3. In his moving book, *Lament for a Son*, Nicholas Wolterstorff (a highly-regarded Christian philosopher) writes about the death of his twenty-five-year-old son, Eric, in a mountain-climbing accident:

   > Job's friends tried out on him their answer. "God did it, Job; he was the agent of your children's death. He did it because of some wickedness in you; he did it to punish you. Nothing indeed in your public life would seem to merit such retribution; it must then be something in your private inner life. Tell us what it is, Job. Confess."
   >
   > The writer of Job refuses to say that God views the lives and deaths of children as cats-o'-nine tails with which to lacerate parents.
   >
   > I have no explanation. I can do nothing else than endure in the face of this deepest and most painful of mysteries. I believe in God the Father Almighty, maker of heaven and earth and resurrecter of Jesus Christ. I also believe that my son's life was cut off in its prime. I cannot fit these pieces together. I am at a loss, I have read the theodicies produced to justify the ways of God to man. I find them unconvincing. To the most agonized questions I have ever asked I do not know the answer. I do not know why God would watch him fall. I do not know why God would watch me wounded. I cannot even guess....
   >
   > I am not angry but baffled and hurt. My wound is an unanswered question. The wounds of all humanity are an unanswered question.[3]

Wolterstorff is not angry with God; he is baffled and hurt. He doesn't understand. In your loss, which perspective best describes how you dealt with this issue:

- ❑ There are deep mysteries in the universe that confound our minds.
- ❑ Faith is not dependent upon understanding all of what happens.
- ❑ Easy answers are not so easy when life caves in.
- ❑ Love is at the heart of the universe, even when we cannot see it.
- ❑ As we weep, so too God weeps.
- ❑ To probe such issues is impossible and best left alone.
- ❑ Other:_____.

4. Close with a time of silent or conversational prayer thanking God for bringing you together as a group and asking him to help you grow through this process.

**REFERENCE NOTES**

**21:1-26** In this passage Job responds to the comments (recorded in chapter 20) of one of his friends, Zophar. Zophar suggests that Job's suffering must be the result of some act of greed (or other hidden evil) that Job had long nurtured. Zophar's view is that suffering is God's punishment against evildoers. Since Job is suffering, he must have done evil. Job rejects that argument by asserting that it is not true to life: there are plenty of obviously evil people in the world who live to a ripe old age and never experience severe hardship. Likewise, there are many people who pursue God's ways all their lives and die "never having enjoyed anything good" (v.25).

**21:2-3 consolation/mock on**. His friends were the most helpful to Job when they simply sat in silence with him (2:13). When they attempted to explain his suffering, they actually intensified it by their assumption that his suffering reflects God's judgment upon some sin that he needs to acknowledge. Since Job is convinced that for his whole life he has sought to honor God (and God himself says this is so in 1:8, where he declares Job "blameless and upright"), their words—far from being consoling—only serve to mock his sincerity and integrity.

**21:4 Is my complaint directed to man?** The answer to this rhetorical question is "No." Job's argument is with a God who is silent in the face of grave injustice.

**21:5 Look at me and be astonished**. Job's situation should cause his friends to be shocked into reconsidering their doctrinally neat position (that suffering is the result of sin). These are men who know Job. They should know better than to insist there must be a hidden, secret sin in his life that merits such distress.

**21:6 I am terrified**. Previously, Job probably shared the views of his friends that suffering was the result of God's judgment upon sin. Now, the security of that formula has been shattered. Job no longer knows what to think. His understanding of God has been shown to be inadequate. Part of his distress is that he does not know how to interpret his experience.

**21:7 Why do the wicked live on?** In the language of the OT, "the wicked" are not necessarily terribly evil people, but those who live their lives without regard for God and his ways. **growing old and increasing**. Job makes the point that many deliberately godless people experience all the blessings of life that popular theology taught was the privilege only of the godly.

[1]Doug Manning, *Don't Take My Grief Away*, San Francisco, Harper & Row, 1979, p. 60.
[2]C.S. Lewis, *A Grief Observed*, pp. 7–9.
[3]Nicholas Wolterstorff, *Lament for a Son*, p. 67-68.

# Denial

**OBJECTIVE** | **The aims of the two sessions in this chapter are:**

- To consider the various ways in which denial shows itself in times of grief.
- To examine through a case study the benefits and the dangers of denial.
- To study a passage in which one of Job's friends attempts to deny Job's pain.

---

| **1** | **Examining the Issue** | 60 Minutes |

**OPEN**

**LEADER:**
Go around the group and, beginning with yourself, let each person respond *briefly* to the first question. Do the same for each question.

**This Can't Be Happening...(15 minutes).**

Think back to when you were a teenager and experienced what you then considered to be a significant loss. Perhaps it was breaking up with a special girlfriend or boyfriend, failing an important test, losing your good looks to acne, or tripping and falling in that big race. Today this adolescent pain may even seem humorous, but back then it wasn't!

1. Briefly describe this painful event to the group.

2. How did you respond to it?
   - ❏ I couldn't believe it; I just stood there in shock.
   - ❏ I shrugged it off as though it didn't matter.
   - ❏ I went out and did something dumb.
   - ❏ I made a joke out of it.
   - ❏ I went inward in numb pain.
   - ❏ I told my friends about it and they helped me.
   - ❏ I cried.
   - ❏ I simply refused to accept what was said or done.
   - ❏ I pretended it didn't happen.
   - ❏ I blamed it on someone (or something) else.
   - ❏ I faced it directly and took my lumps.

3. Do you remember what helped you make it through this painful event?

**CONSIDER**

**Consider the following information about the role of denial in the grief process (5 minutes).**

"No . . . it can't be."

Whether a writer sits stunned before her word processor as a power outage suddenly erases hours of work, or a father stands

**LEADER:**
**Present this material while the group follows along in the text.**

in shock before a police officer who reports that his son has been arrested for robbery, this is our first response. "This can't be happening to me" is the standard reaction of most people when they experience a significant loss. Shock is that feeling of unreality that surrounds the bad news. It feels like you are in a bad dream that you want to go away. You still walk and talk and otherwise function, but you are in a daze. Shock is our first line of defense against tragedy.

One woman, when informed by the hospital that her mother had just died, hung up the phone and proceeded to go shopping just as she had planned to do that day. Later on, she was astonished by how easily she put the news of her mother's death out of her mind by following her planned routine. She was in a state of shock.

Shock is normal and automatic. It may last for only a few seconds, or for hours (or even a few weeks). It is a psychological safeguard that provides people a much-needed way to buy some time as they try to grasp the significance of what has happened to them.

There is a problem, however, when people fail to move beyond shock. It is as if they refuse to confront and accept what has happened to them. Shock has become denial.

Denial is, at its heart, refusing to face up to the new reality. But denial is not just refusing to accept what has happened. Often denial is refusing to own our grief. Denial is expressed in a variety of ways:

- **Some people simply refuse to face the facts of their situation.** A man lies in a hospital bed after a major accident. Despite his sedated condition, he overhears a newscaster on a television set in an adjoining room reporting on the accident. "Two people died and one was hospitalized and is in critical condition." The man knows he was the only one hospitalized, but, despite the fact that he cannot move his legs, he thinks to himself, "But I'm not in critical condition." In the 1989 movie, *Dead Poets' Society*, a boy commits suicide. When his parents discover the boy's body, the mother screams, "No. He's all right. He's all right."

- **Some people just avoid the subject.** This is denial by neglect. The idea is that if you don't talk about something, it isn't real. For example, some people feel great pressure to "get over" their grief in order to "prove their faith." So a month after the funeral, they stand up in church and testify how they have victory over grief. However, no matter what they say (and sincerely feel), grief over the loss of a loved one is not dealt with that quickly, no matter how much faith one has. The grief has just been buried for the moment. (N.B.: it is God who made us creatures capable of experiencing grief. Getting over grief is not a test of faith.)

- **Some people deny a painful event by throwing themselves into situations that keep them from experiencing the pain.** After a divorce or the death of a spouse, many people find themselves working extremely long hours as a way of avoiding the new reality at home. Others start drinking heavily or use other substances as a way of sedating their painful feelings.

Denial is quite normal and even necessary. However, sometimes a person can become "stuck" in this stage of grief in such a way that serious problems result, either for that person or for those who relate to him or her. Denial can be dangerous:

- A woman is told by her doctor that her heart condition is such that she must go on a restricted diet and start a regular exercise program. Unable to face the fact of her heart disease, she ignores the doctor's warning and continues in her present life-style, regardless of its dangers to her health.

- A man who is dying refuses to make the necessary legal and financial arrangements that death entails. He keeps assuring his family that he is getting better, despite what the doctors are saying. Unwilling to accept that death is near, he fails to make vital decisions. The result is that he leaves family members in the potentially explosive situation of deciding what "Daddy would have wanted" without the benefit of his instructions.

- A man whose wife has confronted him (with issues she feels are seriously undermining their marriage) simply refuses to hear her. "She'll get over it" is what he tells himself. His denial may only be broken when his wife actually files for divorce.

Not all denial is bad. It can be a good and natural way of dealing with only one aspect of a loss at a time. It is not necessary to deal with all the implications—financial, emotional, social—of the loss of a spouse when the business at hand is getting through the funeral. Denial can be God's way of letting "today's anxieties be sufficient for today." However, the danger of denial occurs when we postpone dealing with the realities associated with our grief when they should be confronted. In such situations, loving confrontation (and perhaps counseling) may be needed to help the person face what has happened and adjust to the new reality that surrounds him or her.

**DISCUSS**

**Discuss with the group your response to the following case study (15 minutes).**

### Mike ════════════════════

It had come as a shock to Mike. He knew things had been a little strained with his wife, Laura. She had been upset for a while now. But the discussion—or announcement—at breakfast seemed out of the blue. Everything was fairly normal as he sat at the table reading the morning paper until Laura, who was typically quiet at breakfast, broke the silence with the words, "Mike, I'm leaving you. I've thought about it for a long time, and I'm leaving today. When you get home from work, I'll be gone."

Mike just stared at her. She turned and left the room. Mike, not at all sure what to think, put on his coat and went to work.

The bizarre feelings at breakfast gave way to the comfortable sense of camaraderie at work. He completed his morning responsibilities as usual, and enjoyed the light banter over the lunch table. Mike entered into the discussion about the World Series, the upcoming election, and the jokes about the new guy in the office. He did not mention what Laura had said, even to his friend who happened to ask how she was. "Oh, she's fine, thanks. I'll tell her you asked about her," was all he said.

After work, Mike drove home. When he entered the house, silence was all that greeted him. He watched the evening news and then made himself some dinner, working on the paper's crossword puzzle as he ate. Later, he sat down to watch the Series game. Then it hit him.

Mike began to sob, fighting it all the while, but he could't resist the feelings of fear and hurt that were forcing their way out. He went to the phone and called his pastor. "John," he said, "Laura's gone. I really need to talk to someone."

1. Which forms of denial characterized Mike's response?
   - ❏ refused to face the facts
   - ❏ occupied himself with the trivial
   - ❏ carried on his normal routine
   - ❏ used humor
   - ❏ worked long hours
   - ❏ started drinking heavily
   - ❏ used religion compulsively
   - ❏ failed to notice the key facts
   - ❏ started behaving irrationally

2. If you were in Mike's situation, which forms of denial (if any) would you most likely have used?

3. In what ways might the denial that day have helped him finally face what was happening?

4. How did his short-term denial hurt him? What potential problems could you anticipate if Mike had continued over the long term to avoid talking about the situation?

**RESPOND**

**LEADER:**
This exercise will give people time to share more about their grief experience.

**Split into groups of four and discuss the following questions (25 minutes).**

1. Think about the loss you experienced:
   - What do you remember about your initial reaction?
   - Of the forms of denial mentioned here, which ones have you experienced?
   - What helped you move past denial in your particular situation?

2. This meeting may have brought up some painful memories. Use the final few minutes to pray for one another, in light of the feelings that have been shared. You can either pray brief prayers out loud or pray in silence for one another. You might want to end with a group hug as a way of showing love and support for one another.

| 2 | **Bible Study** | 60 Minutes |

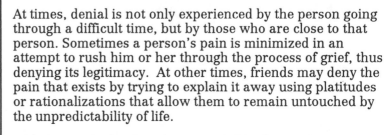

**OPEN**

**Sharing our Stories (15 minutes).**

During this time ask one or two members of the group to share in some detail his or her story of loss. No response is required from the group except to listen attentively. Conclude the sharing by spending a few moments in prayer as a group.

**CONSIDER**

**Read this introduction before you study the passage.**

**LEADER:**
Present this material while the group follows along in the text.

At times, denial is not only experienced by the person going through a difficult time, but by those who are close to that person. Sometimes a person's pain is minimized in an attempt to rush him or her through the process of grief, thus denying its legitimacy. At other times, friends may deny the pain that exists by trying to explain it away using platitudes or rationalizations that allow them to remain untouched by the unpredictability of life.

Bildad, one of Job's friends, responds like this. In the first of his three speeches in the Book of Job, he demonstrates that he has no patience with Job's complaining. Instead, he counsels Job to face the obvious fact of God's judgment upon him, straighten out his life, and get on with things. Had Bildad simply remained silent as he had done in the beginning, he would have been far more comforting!

In this chapter, Bildad appeals to long-standing religious tradition as a way of accounting for Job's situation. In so doing, he effectively tries to deny the reality, significance, and uniqueness of Job's pain.

**READ**

**Read the passage below. Use the reference notes that follow to enhance your understanding of the text (5 minutes).**

**LEADER:**
Allow group members time on their own to read the text and reference notes.

*¹Then Bildad the Shuhite replied:*

*²"How long will you say such things?*
*Your words are a blustering wind.*
*³Does God pervert justice?*
*Does the Almighty pervert what is right?*
*⁴When your children sinned against him,*
*he gave them over to the penalty of their sin.*
*⁵But if you will look to God*
*and plead with the Almighty,*
*⁶if you are pure and upright,*
*even now he will rouse himself on your behalf*
*and restore you to your rightful place.*
*⁷Your beginnings will seem humble,*
*so prosperous will your future be.*

*8"Ask the former generations*
*and find out what their fathers learned,*
*9for we were born only yesterday and know nothing,*
*and our days on earth are but a shadow.*
*10Will they not instruct you and tell you?*
*Will they not bring forth words from their*
*understanding?*
*11Can papyrus grow tall where there is no marsh?*
*Can reeds thrive without water?*
*12While still growing and uncut,*
*they wither more quickly than grass.*
*13Such is the destiny of all who forget God;*
*so perishes the hope of the godless.*
*14What he trusts in is fragile;*
*what he relies on is a spider's web.*
*15He leans on his web, but it gives way;*
*he clings to it, but it does not hold.*
*16He is like a well-watered plant in the sunshine,*
*spreading its shoots over the garden;*
*17it entwines its roots around a pile of rocks*
*and looks for a place among the stones.*
*18But when it is torn from its spot,*
*that place disowns it and says, 'I never saw you.'*
*19Surely its life withers away,*
*and from the soil other plants grow.*

*20"Surely God does not reject a blameless man*
*or strengthen the hands of evildoers.*
*21He will yet fill your mouth with laughter*
*and your lips with shouts of joy.*
*22Your enemies will be clothed in shame,*
*and the tents of the wicked will be no more."*

*Job 8*

**DISCUSS**

Discuss the passage with your group using the questions which follow (20 minutes).

1. What does the passage (as a whole and in particular verse 2) reveal about Bildad's feelings toward Job's concerns? In his eyes, Job is:
   - ❏ A hypocrite who is pretending to be righteous
   - ❏ A person who asks questions he shouldn't
   - ❏ Self-deceived and unwilling to face his real situation
   - ❏ A poor guy who got it in the neck and doesn't know why
   - ❏ A windbag
   - ❏ Unwilling to accept what the wise men of Israel taught
   - ❏ All talk, no show
   - ❏ A person who has left God
   - ❏ "Pure, upright, blameless"

Discuss why you made the choices that you did.

2. What is the issue that Bildad feels is at stake in Job's questioning?
   - ❏ The wisdom of the ages
   - ❏ Bildad's own assumptions about how God operates
   - ❏ Job's refusal to admit his sin
   - ❏ Whether a person has the right to question God
   - ❏ The fact of God's goodness

3. In verses 8-10, Bildad uses the authority of the wise men of Israel as the basis for his comments. How does this view protect Bildad from facing the fact that he too might one day suffer as Job does?

4. One woman who gave birth to a baby with a severe birth defect was told that this must have happened because of some sin in her life. Given the information in verses 4-6, how do you think Bildad would feel about such a statement? How do you feel about such an explanation?

**RESPOND**

**Wrap up your discussion with these questions (20 minutes).**

1. What modern counterparts to "the wisdom of Bildad" have you encountered when dealing with pain? Do you see any echoes of Bildad in the way you might have counseled others in the past?

2. What view would Bildad likely have of you and your situation, as compared to Job's? How would you respond to a friend like Bildad?

3. This meeting may have brought up some painful memories. Use the final few minutes to pray for one another, in light of the feelings that have been shared. You can either pray brief prayers out loud or pray in silence for one another. You might want to end with a group hug as a way of showing love and support for one another.

**REFERENCE NOTES**

**8:1-22** In chapters 4-5, one of Job's friends, Eliphaz, suggested that Job's distress over his suffering was inappropriate. After all, Job should recognize that "those who plow evil and those who sow trouble will reap it" (4:8). Instead of complaining, Eliphaz says that Job ought to turn to God, thankful for this time of correction (5:17). Job does not respond to Eliphaz' comments, but instead laments his situation all the more in chapters 6-7. Now it's Bildad's turn, and he rebukes Job by essentially calling him a windbag (8:2)!

**8:3** Bildad is concerned that Job's questions reflect a lack of respect for God's justice, and so he leaps to God's defense. But Job had not doubted God's justice; he simply expressed concern over the fact that he could not see it in operation in his case.

**8:4 When your children sinned.** Given his conviction that tragedy is God's judgment upon sin, Bildad's only conclusion is that Job's children must have had some secret sin that accounted for their fate.

**8:5-7** Bildad's "comfort" is conditional and insensitive to Job's pain. He asserts that if Job will now turn to God and start living right, then God will make everything better.

**8:8-19** In support of his theology of strict retribution, Bildad appeals to the tradition of the fathers, an irrefutable source of authority for people in the Ancient Near East. His point is clear: "As surely as effect follows cause in the natural world, suffering is the result of sin in the life of man" (Gordis). As part of this appeal to authority, Bildad retells an ancient parable (vv.11-19). The point of the parable is that the destruction of an apparently healthy plant is an illustration of the sudden downfall that secretly wicked people will experience.

**8:8 the former generations**. This refers not to the immediately preceding generations, but to the legendary, heroic figures like Noah and Enoch (who lived extraordinarily long lives in the distant past). In direct opposition to today's culture (in which new and creative ideas are viewed as the most valid), the belief at that time was that the "closer one lived to the origins of the cosmos, the greater the contact with the source of wisdom" (Habel).

**8:13** Just as papyrus needs a continual source of moisture to survive, so people need to draw upon a continuous source of life. Those who cut themselves off from God cut themselves off from the very source of their nurture. While they may initially sprout up, they (like a papyrus reed in a dry land) will quickly wither. **hope**. They wither because they have no hope. Hope is a "source of renewal an individual needs in order to survive and flourish in the face of disaster" (Habel).

**8:14-15** The metaphor of the withered plant gives way to the image of a person trying to support himself or herself by grasping onto a spider's web. The point is that there is no security apart from God.

**8:16-19** This is a recapitulation of the point made in verses 11-15. The wicked appear like a "well-watered plant" firmly rooted in a garden, but such a person will be torn up, disowned, and wither away while other people blossom in his or her former place.

**8:20-22** Bildad summarizes his case to Job by inviting him to become a blameless man. Job has been declared blameless by God (1:8). Part of the agony Job experiences is that the traditional interpretations of such events simply do not fit his experience. Bildad's approach is simplistic, moralistic, and totally inappropriate to the struggles with which Job is wrestling.

# Anger

**OBJECTIVE** | **The aims of the two sessions in this chapter are:**

- To consider the role anger plays in the grief process.
- To examine some ways of dealing with anger.
- To consider the implications for ourselves of a passage from Job where he expresses anger at God.

| **1** | **Examining the Issue** | **60 Minutes** |

**OPEN**

**When I Get Angry...(15 minutes).**

**LEADER:**
Go around the group and, beginning with yourself, let each person respond *briefly* to the first question. Do the same for each question.

1. People have different ways of dealing with anger. When you get angry, what do you do typically:

   ☐ What? Me angry?  ☒ I sulk.
   ☐ I blow up.  ☐ I blame others.
   ☐ I quietly count to ten.  ☐ I exercise.
   ☐ I yell a lot, but it's all just hot air.
   ☐ I deal directly with the source of my anger in a constructive way.
   ☐ I hold my breath and turn purple.
   ☐ I take it out on my kids or dog.
   ☒ I do a slow burn.
   ☐ I just push it away and slap on a plastic smile.
   ☐ I assume I'm probably over-reacting.
   ☐ I get cutting and sarcastic.
   ☐ I act like there is no problem.

2. Think about the things that tend to tick you off. Which one got your goat recently:

   ☐ traffic  ☒ people who are late
   ☐ your dog (cat, parrot, etc)  ☐ government
   ☐ your spouse  ☐ celebrities
   ☐ your job  ☒ crime
   ☐ clerks in stores  ☒ injustice
   ☐ mechanics  ☐ inconsiderate people
   ☐ your children  ☐ in-laws
   ☐ the media  ☐ neighbors

   Share the incident with the group.

3. How is your way of dealing with anger like (or unlike) that of your parents?

**CONSIDER**

**Consider the following information about the role of anger in the grief process (5 minutes).**

**LEADER:**
Present this material while the group follows along in the text.

Once the reality of a hard situation begins to press in on us, we get angry. Often this anger is our way of covering up or expressing the conflicting emotions that erupt in us during times of loss (some of which we are unaware of; some of which we do not understand).

Our anger gets pointed in various directions: at the person whose loss we are grieving, at God, at ourselves, or at other people (whether or not they are involved in the problem). Sometimes our anger is focused on someone who is, for all intents and purposes, an innocent bystander. He or she just happens to be there and happens to give us a "reason" for being angry, no matter how spurious the cause. Listen to these various expressions of anger:

- Joni Erikson Tada, a woman paralyzed as a teenager by a diving accident, says that even now (despite the fact that she has accepted this tragedy and has understood that because of it she now has a national ministry to the handicapped), she still experiences times of loathing against the very wheelchair that allows her a degree of mobility.

- Some automobile insurance companies raise their rates for people who have gone through a divorce because statistically, in the first months after a divorce, certain people tend to take out their anger behind the wheel of a car.

- An elderly man whose wife is dying experiences terrible guilt over the feelings of anger against her that surface within him. He knows it is certainly not her fault that she is dying, yet the question "Why is she doing this to me?" comes to his mind over and over again.

The ways we express anger vary:

• **Some people react directly.** One writer records the story of how a man attacked and beat the doctor who announced the death of the man's brother at the scene of an accident. This is, of course, an extreme case!

• **Others express their anger indirectly.** They complain: "The nurses are stupid." "The doctor doesn't listen." "The minister's no good because he didn't read a psalm." "What fool would drive on that road at night anyway?" This is unfocused anger. This is anger looking for an object to which it can attach itself. This sort of anger is often the result of feelings of powerlessness. It is a way of reacting to the apparent irrationality of events.

• **Others cannot face their anger when it arises and only express it well after the fact.** Consider the response of two sisters to their parents' divorce. The younger one expressed her anger directly at the time of the divorce. At bedtime she would say: "It's your fault that Daddy isn't with me now." The older sister said little, but three years later her anger came out in a harmful relationship she developed with a boy that mirrored the destructive patterns that broke her parents apart.

• **Other people express their anger through self-destructive behavior.** This is a form of self-anger, stemming from the fact that they blame themselves for failing to alter the course of events. One person becomes deeply depressed. Another develops a severe rash which is diagnosed as a stress-related disease. Others indulge in dangerous (or socially unacceptable) behavior like drunkenness, reckless driving, or other adult versions of a child's tantrum.

As hard as it is to deal with anger (for the person feeling it and for those around him or her), *anger is a healthy expression of real emotion*. Rather than repressing or ignoring it, people at this stage of grief will find it more helpful to:

• **Admit they are angry.** This is more difficult than it sounds, because most of us have been conditioned to cover up our anger with more acceptable emotions (or with reasons). "I'm not angry, I'm just perturbed that the doctor is so slow," or "I was all right until Paul said such-and-such." What we should be saying is something like: "I really am in turmoil. I feel so angry, and I don't know what to do."

• **Reflect on their anger.** What really lies behind the outburst or the behavior? This is especially helpful when anger at a loss has been delayed or denied but begins to seep out in irrational ways. One man, after experiencing both a divorce and the death of his mother within two months, found himself blowing up at his children more and more often over inconsequential matters. In considering his irrational outbursts, he realized that the hurt and anger he had suppressed (in order to be a good model for the children) was now coming out in unfair ways against them. "The anger I am feeling is not really because of my children, it is my anger over the divorce."

• **Look for meaning behind the emotion.** We are angry over the loss of a loved one because of all the implications for us. We resent being left alone; we resent being left with bills to pay; we miss all the benefits we experienced from being in partnership with our spouse. Anger exists because of the tremendous worth of the person whom we have lost. Once understood, this anger can be a touchstone to remind us to value and appreciate the memory of our loved one and to express appreciation more readily for the other significant people in our lives.

• **Act out their anger in a safe, healthful way**. This might mean keeping journals to allow feelings to pour out, regardless of whether such feelings are "acceptable" or "good." They might go on brisk walks when they sense their anger surfacing, punch a punching bag, visit a counselor or join a grief support group. Ask a friend: "Could I ask you a favor? Can I blow off some steam with you?"

• **Let the anger go**. This is not the same as denying or repressing anger. Rather, it is a choice to move past the hurt so that it is not allowed to dominate and damage one's life. This is only possible when anger has been accepted, reflected upon, and acted out in some way. "I really have lost Jane, and boy, does it hurt, but I'm going to make it."

Being with those who are working through their anger can be difficult. But it is during such times they need us the most. A helpful way to cope with such people's anger is suggested in an article in the Christian Medical Society Journal (Fall 1974):

When anger is expressed at us, we ought to absorb it. Arguing or quieting the bereaved may make guilt even worse and emotion more difficult to express. When hostility is expressed at others, we can respond with a simple statement of fact. "From what I observed, the pastor did all that he could." Perhaps at a later time when life has become more stable it might be helpful to discuss the matter in a more probing way, but not now.

**DISCUSS**

**Discuss with the group your response to the following questions (15 minutes).**

1. Dealing with conflict and anger is a normal part of human relationships. In your everyday life, how do you typically express your anger to others?
   - ❏ I'm pretty direct. I put it on the table.
   - ☒ I hate having to deal with conflict. I tend to get passive on the outside and be in turmoil on the inside.
   - ❏ I get visibly angry, but express that anger at other people or things—not the ones I'm really angry with.
   - ❏ I never seem to get angry.
   - ❏ I'm usually at fault, so I feel guilty and attempt to apologize.
   - ❏ Anger hurts more than it helps, so I attempt to smooth the waters.

2. If your spouse, children, or siblings were asked to label your way of dealing with conflict or anger, how would they characterize you? (Choose from the options in question one or make up your own.)

3. Each style of dealing with anger is a two-sided coin: it has a positive and a negative face to it. When is your way of dealing with conflict and anger positive for you and the situation, and when is it negative for you and the situation?

**RESPOND**

**Split into groups of four and discuss the following questions (25 minutes).**

1. In terms of the way you are dealing with your loss, put yourself somewhere on the scale and explain your response to the group.

| | | | |
|---|---|---|---|
| Not felt any anger yet | Just beginning to understand the anger part | I'm right in the middle of dealing with my anger | I've already processed the anger |

2. When we are grieving, our anger gets directed in various ways. Where have you tended to direct your anger:
   - ☐ at myself
   - ☐ at my family
   - ☐ at God
   - ☐ at a specific person
   - ☐ at others in general
   - ☐ at my church
   - ☐ at my loved ones

3. What are some constructive ways that you have found to deal with your anger as you have gone through the grief process?

4. In terms of dealing with your present loss, which one of the suggestions for coping with anger seems the most applicable to you? Why?

**LEADER:**
Close with a time of prayer in which the group thanks God for one another and for the fact that he is not put off by our anger.

5. What is one thing you have especially appreciated about these times together so far? What has been most helpful? Why?

| 2 | **Bible Study** | 60 Minutes |

**OPEN**

Sharing our Stories (15 minutes).

During this time ask one or two members of the group to share in some detail his or her story of loss. No response is required from the group, except to listen attentively. Conclude the sharing by spending a few moments in prayer as a group.

**CONSIDER**

**LEADER:**
Present this material while the group follows along in the text.

Read this introduction before you study the passage.

In the last session, we read Bildad's scathing rebuke of Job in chapter 8. In this session, we'll look at the comments of Job in chapter 7 that elicited Bildad's strong response.

In chapter 7, Job is angry at God. He is angry at God for what seems to be God's inability (or unwillingness) to do anything to alleviate his misery. In Job's view, God simply allows the intense suffering to go on and on unabated. As a result, Job erupts in frustration and anger against God. As it turns out, God is able to absorb all of Job's anger. At the end of the book he commends Job (42:7-8), though he also shows Job that Job's view of him is inadequate.

As you read the following chapter, remember that Job would not have been angry at God if God had not been central in his life. Even Job's anger is ample testimony to his deep love for God. If God had been merely "an idea" to Job (or if God had been conceived of as an "impersonal force" in the universe), God probably would not have been the target of his anger.

**READ**

**LEADER:**
Allow group members time on their own to read the text and reference notes.

Read the passage below. Use the reference notes that follow to enhance your understanding of the text (5 minutes).

¹*"Does not man have hard service on earth?*
*Are not his days like those of a hired man?*
²*Like a slave longing for the evening shadows,*
*or a hired man waiting eagerly for his wages,*
³*so I have been allotted months of futility,*
*and nights of misery have been assigned to me.*
⁴*When I lie down I think, 'How long before I get up?'*
*The night drags on, and I toss till dawn.*
⁵*My body is clothed with worms and scabs,*
*my skin is broken and festering.*

⁶*"My days are swifter than a weaver's shuttle,*
*and they come to an end without hope....*

¹¹*"Therefore I will not keep silent;*
*I will speak out in the anguish of my spirit,*
*I will complain in the bitterness of my soul.*

*¹²Am I the sea, or the monster of the deep,*
*that you put me under guard?*
*¹³When I think my bed will comfort me*
*and my couch will ease my complaint,*
*¹⁴even then you frighten me with dreams*
*and terrify me with visions,*
*¹⁵so that I prefer strangling and death,*
*rather than this body of mine.*
*¹⁶I despise my life; I would not live forever.*
*Let me alone; my days have no meaning....*

*²⁰If I have sinned, what have I done to you,*
*O watcher of men?*
*Why have you made me your target?*
*Have I become a burden to you?*
*²¹Why do you not pardon my offenses*
*and forgive my sins?*
*For I will soon lie down in the dust;*
*you will search for me, but I will be no more."*

*Job 7:1–6, 11–16, 20–21*

**DISCUSS**

**Discuss the passage with your group using the questions which follow (20 minutes).**

1. Scan the chapter for Job's descriptions of his circumstances. What is happening to Job physically, emotionally, and spiritually that accounts for his anger?

2. How do you feel about Job's anger at God? Explain your response:
   - ❑ embarrassed?          ❑ disturbed?
   - ❑ amazed?               ❑ upset?
   - ❑ angry at Job?         ❑ angry at God?

3. Is Job's complaint against God more like one of a man distressed over the fact that his beloved has neglected him, or more like one of a man terrified that his enemy is overpowering him? Why do you think so?

4. In a book written by a Christian counselor, the author says that Job's anger reflected a sinful, demanding spirit that refused to accept and trust God's sovereignty over the life. Other Christian counselors say that it was appropriate for Job to express his anger and frustration at God over the intolerable circumstances. With which opinion do you agree (or is there another approach that you see)? Explain.

5. How would you defend God against Job's charges? How would you defend Job in his anger against God?

6. What are the positive lessons that you learn about suffering from this chapter ?

**RESPOND** | **Wrap up your discussion with these questions (20 minutes).**

1. If your under-your-breath conversations during hard times were monitored, what would they likely reveal about you?
   - ☐ lots of self-criticism, berating myself
   - ☐ lots of pep-talk, encouraging myself
   - ☐ cursing and a smouldering anger at God
   - ☐ sarcastic comebacks against people who tried to help
   - ☐ pleas for help
   - ☐ other:_____

2. When have you felt that at least some of Job's description in 7:1-6 was your story?

3. Joni Erikson Tada says there is a great difference between crying out "Why?" to God with open hands, and making the same cry with a closed fist. Which fits the way you respond to God during hard times?

4. In your experience, when you get angry at God, what is the usual outcome?
   - ☐ I calm down, but the anger gets stored away until next time.
   - ☐ I give up, because God is bigger than I am.
   - ☐ I typically have a change in perspective, seeing things in a different light.
   - ☐ I use it against God. It's why I don't believe in God much anymore.
   - ☐ I don't get angry at God; I get angry at someone or something else.
   - ☐ It somehow gives way to a sense of his love and presence in the midst of my pain. He can take my anger.
   - ☐ Other:_____.

5. Religious people can hold on to subtle anger at God, even while faithfully performing all their religious and spiritual obligations. What do you see as the danger in that approach?

**LEADER:**
Close with a time of prayer in which the group thanks God for one another and for the fact that he is not put off by our anger.

6. What do you need to help you get past either blatant or quiet anger at God over the hard times in your life?

7. What is one thing that you have appreciated most about these times together so far? What has been most helpful? Why?

**REFERENCE NOTES** | **7:1-21** In chapter 6, Job expressed his frustration at Eliphaz's insensitivity to his pain. In this chapter, he expresses his frustration at God, whom he feels is relentless in causing his agony. This chapter is a poem with three parts: Part I consists of verses 1-8, Part II of verses 9-16, and Part III of verses 17-21.

**7:1-8** The first stanza uses the image of a slave to emphasize the misery and oppression under which people live out their futile lives.

**7:1 hard service**. This word was used for forced military service and for forced labor (such as when a king would conscript workers for a project). Some of the pagan religions of the time viewed humanity as laborers created to perform the work of the gods. **a hired man**. These were day laborers who were paid only a subsistence wage. They had no security nor any claim upon the loyalty of their employer.

**7:2 slave/hired man**. Both classes of workers were involved in constant work which was of no benefit to them personally. The slave's only hope lay in the evening shadows when he could rest, and the hired man's in the paltry wage he would receive at the end of the day.

**7:3 months**. There is no mention in the Book of Job itself as to how long Job's suffering lasted. Jewish tradition speculates that it was anywhere from one to seven years. **of futility**. Literally, "emptiness, worthlessness." His lot is even worse than that of a hired man. At least a hired man receives some wage at the end of the day, but for Job there is nothing.

**7:4-5** Whereas even a slave finds relief from his misery at night, Job is tormented by wounds, by itching, and by sores to such a degree that sleep escapes him. Both day and night his misery overwhelms him.

**7:9-16** In this second stanza, the brevity and insignificance of life is emphasized by comparing life to a cloud.

**7:11** Eliphaz had encouraged Job to be pious before God as his only hope of being restored (4:6). In contrast, Job defies traditional piety by crying out in his anguish to God. He is angry at God for the hardships he faces and he will no longer refrain from challenging God and calling him unfair, cruel, and uncaring.

**7:12 the sea/the monster of the deep**. Powerful agents of chaos which threatened creation. God's power was seen in that he alone could restrain and conquer them (i.e., Ps 74:13-14; Isa 27:1). Job's complaint is full of irony: "How could I, a mere man, be such a threat to you that I need to be treated like your powerful cosmic enemies?"

**7:13-15** The nightmares that torment him make sleep a time when God assaults him in a new way.

**7:16** In Job's second taunt to God, he rejects any offer of longer life (or even eternal life). Who wants to live at all if it means being constantly afflicted by God in this way? Job's only wish is that God would leave him alone and let him die.

**7:20 If I have sinned**. This is probably intended to be a hypothetical question, for Job is not aware of how he could have offended God to such an extent as to merit this punishment. **O watcher of men**. The fact that God kept watch over Israel was meant to be a source of comfort (Dt 32:10; Ps 121). Instead Job sees it as a divine threat, imagining that God pries and probes into all aspects of a person's life, looking for some reason to punish that person. **your target**. From Job's perspective, not only is God impartially "watching" him, he is actively out to get him! **a burden to you?** In verses 1-2, humanity's "burden" was having to live as God's slave; here, God's burden is having to put up with the people he created, especially Job.

**7:21** The final taunt to God is a mock request for forgiveness for whatever horrible sin Job supposedly must have committed. It is as if he said, "Isn't it your place to forgive sinners? So why don't you do it and relieve me of my sufferings? After all, I will soon be dead and you'll have no opportunity to do so then." **lie down in the dust**. This draws together the images of Job's tormented sleep (vv.4, 13-14) and the dust that cakes and devours his body (v.5–see note). Soon, he will lie down for the final time and no one—not even God—will be able to find him anymore.

# Bargaining

**OBJECTIVE**

The aims of the two sessions in this chapter are:

- To examine the role of bargaining in the grief process.
- To consider some of the ways in which people bargain during a time of grief.
- To explore a passage in which Job bargains with God.

| 1 | **Examining the Issue** | 60 Minutes |
|---|---|---|

**OPEN**

**LEADER:**
Go around the group and, beginning with yourself, let each person respond *briefly* to the first question. Do the same for each question.

**Getting My Way (15 minutes).**

1. When you were a child, can you remember a time when you *really* wanted to do something, buy something, or go somewhere, but your parents said no? Share this incident with the group.

2. When your parents refused to allow you to do what you wanted, what did you do?
   - ☐ Scream and shout
   - ☐ Sulk and lock yourself in your room
   - ☐ Plead, beg, and argue
   - ☐ Act real nice for a few days in hopes you could buy them off
   - ☐ A combination of all the above
   - ☐ Just went ahead and did it anyway
   - ☐ Simply went along with their decision
   - ☐ Other: _____

3. Can you recall what effect your reaction had on your parents? Did you get your way? Did your bargaining work?

**CONSIDER**

**Consider the following information about bargaining in the grief process (5 minutes).**

**LEADER:**
Present this material while the group follows along in the text.

Dan could feel the bus slipping out of control and sliding toward the shoulder of the highway. The next thing he remembered was the feeling of the wind and snow swirling around him as he lay on his back next to the open window of the overturned bus. He felt no pain, but he was aware that he could not move his legs. His first thought was, "Dear God, I'll serve you for the rest of my life if only I'm not paralyzed."

Helen was devastated when her husband left her. They had had their problems, to be sure, but she had promised God that she

would be a more loving, caring wife if only God would keep the family together. And she had done her best but *still* her husband left. She couldn't understand why God had not kept his part of the bargain.

John said he would stop drinking if Maggie would stay. This time he meant it, he said. This time he would go to AA. But only if she stayed.

Bargaining. We all know what it is. Things get tough; the pain becomes overwhelming. So we enter, consciously or unconsciously, into some form of negotiation. Generally this is with God; sometimes it is even with the devil. (Literature abounds with stories of people making pacts with the devil.) We bargain with whomever we feel can relieve our situation.

According to Elizabeth Kübler-Ross, bargaining stems from the hope that

> maybe we can succeed in entering into some sort of agreement which may postpone the inevitable happening: "If God has decided to take us from this earth and he did not respond to my angry pleas, he may be more favorable if I ask nicely."… The terminally ill patient [as well as those who are grieving]…knows, from past experiences, that there is a slim chance that he may be rewarded for good behavior and be granted a wish for special services. His wish is most always an extension of life….
>
> The bargaining is really an attempt to postpone; it has to include a prize offered "for good behavior," it also sets a self-imposed "deadline" [e.g., one more performance, the son's wedding], and it includes an implicit promise that [the person] will not ask for more if this one postponement is granted. None of our patients have "kept their promise"; in other words, they are like children who say, "I will never fight my sister again if you let me go." Needless to add, the little boy will fight his sister again…[1]

King David went through this particular stage of grief. His son whom Bathsheba bore fell ill (as had been prophesied). In 2 Samuel 12:16-17 it says: "David pleaded with God for the child. He fasted and went into his house and spent the nights lying on the ground…. He would not eat any food." When the child died, David's servants hesitated to tell him the sad news for fear that "he may do something desperate" (v.18). However, once he heard the news, David went back to normal life. David explained his actions to his servants: "While the child was still alive, I fasted and wept. I thought, 'Who knows? The Lord may be gracious to me and let the child live.' But now that he is dead, why should I fast? Can I bring him back again? I will go to him, but he will not return to me" (2Sa 12:22-23).

Genesis 18 records the story of how Abraham bargained with God. Because of the evil of the city of Sodom, God announced his intention to destroy it. Abraham protested. How could God, the righteous God, destroy the city if there were even as few as fifty righteous people in it? When God agreed that he would not destroy it if fifty were found, Abraham bargained again. How about forty-five? How about forty? How about thirty? And so it went until Abraham succeeded in bargaining God down to ten. It seemed that Abraham was successful in his bargain ...except that there were not even ten righteous people, and so the city was destroyed.

Even Jesus, in his humanity, knew this aspect of grief. In the Garden of Gethsemane on the evening of his arrest, knowing the agony that lay ahead, he was "deeply distressed and troubled." He prayed, "Abba, Father, ... everything is possible for you. Take this cup from me" (Mk 14:33, 36). Jesus did not fast as David did in hopes that God might change his mind. Jesus did not presume, like Abraham, that he understood God's character of righteousness better than God himself. Instead, in the midst of his genuine grief and fear, he entrusted himself to God's will. His prayer ended: "Yet not what I will, but what you will."

Jesus models for us the role of faith in the midst of calamity. He faced squarely what was happening to him. He neither denied nor minimized his situation. And he grieved over what was happening to him. He wanted to escape from it, but he chose to trust God and thus moved through this phase of grief.

In contrast, bargaining is (for most of us) a last ditch attempt to try to control life so that it will go our way. This phase of grief is often the briefest of all the stages. It is the final effort on the part of people to hold on to what is important to them.

And sometimes a reprieve *does* happen. Isaiah 38:1-5 states:

> In those days Hezekiah became ill and was at the point of death. The prophet Isaiah, son of Amoz went to him and said, "This is what the Lord says: Put your house in order, because you are going to die; you will not recover." Hezekiah turned his face to the wall and prayed to the Lord, "Remember, O Lord, how I have walked before you faithfully and with wholehearted devotion and have done what is good in your eyes." And Hezekiah wept bitterly. Then the word of the Lord came to Isaiah: "Go and tell Hezekiah, 'This is what the Lord, the God of your father David, says: I have heard your prayer and seen your tears; I will add fifteen years to your life.'"

Cancers do suddenly go into remission. A wife changes her mind about pursuing a divorce. The insurance company decides, after all, to pay for the loss of your house. The problem is that if people feel that such reprises are somehow related to their bargaining, it can set them up to repeat the stages of denial and anger and bargaining if things once again take a turn for the worse. Bargaining is very human—it may even be a necessary part of the grief process; it is not, however, the way one automatically alters events.

But not every grieving person goes through the bargaining stage, at least not in the way described by Kübler-Ross. She derived her stages of grief by observing those who were dying, not those who were left behind. And while the process is often similar for both sets of people, it is not always identical.

What grieving people will often experience instead of bargaining is the related "If only..." stage: "If only I had insisted that he go to the doctor instead of just suggesting it." "If only I hadn't worried so much about money and we took that vacation she always dreamed of." "If only I'd been a better son." Regrets. Memories of past injuries inflicted (and received). Unresolved issues. Unfullfilled dreams. These are what survivors have to deal with.

Frank Cherry and John James have found that many of those who grieve start to regret the past. They wish for three things: that the past could be *different, better,* or *more.* And this produces guilt. In response, they enshrine those who have died, making them out to be "perfect," refusing to part with any of their clothes or objects. Or they start to take on the traits of the person who has died by getting involved in their hobbies and interests.[2] Such feelings of regret and guilt must be noted for what they are and dealt with in an open, honest way. They are part of coming to terms with our loss.

How do we deal with feelings of regret and guilt? Where there is real guilt over genuine misdeeds, there is no shortcut but to confess such things to God and ask his forgiveness. The New Testament promises that "if we confess our sins, [God] is faithful and just and will forgive us our sins and purify us from all unrighteousness" (1Jn 1:9). This is a powerful promise. As for past regrets, they can be transformed into wisdom. We can learn from our mistakes and so treat others better.

**DISCUSS**

**Discuss with the group your response to the following questions (15 minutes).**

1. Bargaining is not something we do only when we face the death of a loved one (or our own death). We do it all the time. Which of the following forms of bargaining comes closest to your own experience?

- ❏ Officer, I promise never again to go over 55 miles an hour.
- ❏ If you cut the lawn, I'll bake a cake.
- ❏ Look, if you forget about the (_____), then I'll (_____).
- ❏ I won't report the accident to the police if you'll promise to pay for the repairs.
- ❏ If you'll forgive me for talking out of turn at the party, I'll get you that new dress.
- ❏ Dear God, I'll be good if you promise to protect my family from tragedy.
- ❏ If you marry me, I'll make you happy.
- ❏ Other:_____.

2. Which of your bargains worked?

3. If the positive side of bargaining is that we get what we want, what is the negative side? Bargaining:
   - ❏ Gives us the sense that we are in control of our destiny when reality dictates otherwise.
   - ❏ Gives us the wrong view of God as one who can be manipulated.
   - ❏ Fails to prepare us for the inevitable pain that comes to all lives.
   - ❏ Deludes us into thinking that there is no such thing as consequences for our actions.
   - ❏ Makes us into manipulators.
   - ❏ Other:_____.

**RESPOND**

**Split into groups of four and discuss the following questions (25 minutes).**

**LEADER:**
Give each person two minutes to share his or her answers to each part of question 1 and then two minutes to share his or her answers to each part of question 2.

1. In your own dealing with grief:

   - How have you bargained (if you have)? With whom? To what end?
   - What short-range positive benefits did this attempt at bargaining have for you?
   - Were there any long-range negative effects that you are aware of?

2. In your bargaining:

   - Did it work out or not? Explain what happened.
   - How did you cope with that?

3. Are you bargaining with God right now? How? Why?

4. Close by taking a few moments to pray for one another in light of the needs and feelings expressed during the meeting.

| 2 | **Bible Study** | 60 Minutes |

**OPEN**

**Sharing our Stories (15 minutes).**

During this time ask one or two members of the group to share in some detail his or her story of loss. No response is required from the group, except to listen attentively. Conclude the sharing by spending a few moments in prayer as a group.

**CONSIDER**

**Read this introduction before you study the passage.**

**LEADER:**
Present this material while the group follows along in the text.

What Job really wanted from God was "a day in court." After months of unrelieved suffering, he felt that if only he could get God to hear his case, then he would be delivered. "If only..." these are the words that are often the clue that bargaining is in progress.

The horror Job felt was due to the fact that God seemed not to be the least interested in any such bargain. Since Job was sure about his own uprightness, he had no choice but to question God's goodness and care. Was God merely a being with raw power who pursued his own ways, regardless of justice? Ultimately, it was the conviction that God *is* just that prompted Job to persist with his questions and to continue his search for God in the midst of his sufferings. Somehow, someway, he had to get some understanding of what God was doing through all that was going on in his life.

**READ**

**Read the passage below. Use the reference notes that follow to enhance your understanding of the text (5 minutes).**

**LEADER:**
Allow group members time on their own to read the text and reference notes.

*¹Then Job replied:*

*²"Even today my complaint is bitter;*
*his hand is heavy in spite of my groaning.*
*³If only I knew where to find him;*
*if only I could go to his dwelling!*
*⁴I would state my case before him*
*and fill my mouth with arguments.*
*⁵I would find out what he would answer me,*
*and consider what he would say.*
*⁶Would he oppose me with great power?*
*No, he would not press charges against me.*
*⁷There an upright man could present his case before him,*
*and I would be delivered forever from my judge.*

*⁸"But if I go to the east, he is not there;*
*if I go to the west, I do not find him.*

⁹*When he is at work in the north, I do not see him;*
  *when he turns to the south, I catch no glimpse of him.*
¹⁰*But he knows the way that I take;*
  *when he has tested me, I will come forth as gold.*
¹¹*My feet have closely followed his steps;*
  *I have kept to his way without turning aside.*
¹²*I have not departed from the commands of his lips;*
  *I have treasured the words of his mouth more than*
  *my daily bread.*

¹³*"But he stands alone, and who can oppose him?*
  *He does whatever he pleases.*
¹⁴*He carries out his decree against me,*
  *and many such plans he still has in store.*
¹⁵*That is why I am terrified before him;*
  *when I think of all this, I fear him.*
¹⁶*God has made my heart faint;*
  *the Almighty has terrified me.*
¹⁷*Yet I am not silenced by the darkness,*
  *by the thick darkness that covers my face."*

*Job 23*

**DISCUSS**

Discuss the passage with your group using the questions which follow (20 minutes).

1. "Bargaining" can often be seen in "if . . . then" statements. How might you paraphrase Job's bargain here: "If only _____, then _____"?

2. What expectations does Job have, if only he can have a hearing with God?
   - ☐ that God will explain
   - ☐ that God will not overwhelm him
   - ☐ that he will be vindicated
   - ☐ that God will listen to those who are righteous
   - ☐ that God will be shown to be just
   - ☐ that he will be overcome by fear
   - ☐ that God will be shown to be unjust
   - ☐ that God will demonstrate his care

3. What is Job's frustration with the bargain he would like to offer to God (vv.8-9)?

4. What mood change do you sense in verses 13-17? What does Job fear more than all his troubles? What has happened to his confidence in trying to bargain with God for a fair trial?

5. God often seems uninterested in our attempts to bargain with him. Why?
   - ❐ He has our deepest interests in mind already, although we don't always see this clearly.
   - ❐ I disagree, he will bargain.
   - ❐ He is fully with us in our pain already.
   - ❐ He doesn't really care about us.
   - ❐ We can ask, but we must also trust him.
   - ❐ The universe doesn't run that way; stuff just happens.
   - ❐ He is a God of love, not a God of "If you do this, I'll do that."
   - ❐ Other:_____.

**RESPOND**

**Wrap up your discussion with these questions (20 minutes).**

1. "If only …" statements come in many forms when we grieve. Which kind of "if only…" statements have you made (if any)?
   - ❐ If only I had done something different.
   - ❐ If only I had been different.
   - ❐ If only I had been better.
   - ❐ If only I had been more open.
   - ❐ If only _____.

2. Which "if only …" statements have you dealt with? How? Which "if only …" statements are you still dealing with? How?

3. Doug Manning states: "Most of the "if onlys" are not really true. Even the ones that are true are beyond your control. There is nothing you can do to change them."[3] What do you think (or feel) about this assertion?

4. Close by taking a few moments to pray for one another, in light of the needs and feelings expressed during the meeting.

**REFERENCE NOTES**

**23:1-17** Eliphaz has just finished appealing once again for Job to "submit to God and be at peace with him…" and to "return to the Almighty" (22:21-23). However, here in chapter 23, Job does not respond to his friend or to God; instead, he begins a reflection. This is a soliloquy about how difficult it is to return to God when God is hidden! Job longs to present his case to God, because he is convinced that if only he could do so, God would see things his way and end his suffering.

**23:3-4 If only**. Job's bargain is expressed in his wish that he could find God so that he could argue his case with him. "Here Job's courageous honesty is seen at its best. His consuming desire is to come face to face with God (v.3), not by a contrived penance, as Eliphaz recommends, but in fair trial (v.4). Job has abandoned his earlier hesitation and self-mistrust (9:14-20, 32; 13:18). He is now confident that he will be able to state his case persuasively. …What Job is seeking is confirmation from God, in contradiction of what his friends have been saying, that his right relationship with God, which, throughout his whole life, had been grounded in 'the fear of God' and not in the merit of his own good deeds, was unimpaired" (Anderson).

**23:5-7** Job imagines what such a hearing would be like. The fear he once had that God would simply overwhelm him with great power (9:16-19) is largely put aside (v.6a). He expresses a renewed confidence that God, who embodies all that justice means, would not resort to unfair power tactics to oppress him; rather, God would find Job to be righteous.

**23:7 an upright man.** This does not mean that Job believed himself to be perfect. It expresses the fact that Job knew that his wholehearted desire all his life was to honor God. There was no secret evil that he had tried to hide from God. In Psalm 15, the author also spoke about being blameless. He meant the same thing as Job does—namely, that the general tenor of his life was tuned toward putting God's teachings into practice (see also Ps 26). The proof of Job's sincerity is seen in that he dares to approach the One before whom "no godless man would dare come before..." (13:16).

**23:8-9** The frustration for Job is that he is unable to meet with God.

**23:10 he knows the way that I take.** This might also be read: "God knows his way with me" (Anderson). Either way, verse 10 expresses the idea that Job glimpses the fact that his sufferings are not a punishment, but a test of some sort. **the way.** This is "the way" of God's law, which Job has "closely followed" (v.11), from which he has "not departed" (v.12), and which he has "treasured more than my daily bread" (v.12). He embodies the qualities encouraged in Psalm 19:7-11. **I will come forth as gold.** Whereas earlier Job had complained that God seemed to test people for no reason other than to torment them (7:17-18), now he uses the image of a fire (whose purpose is to test the quality of gold). Job "is so convinced of his absolute integrity that he is willing to be tested in the presence of the all-consuming holiness of God" (Habel).

**23:12 more than my daily bread.** Literally, "more than what is required of me." The Hebrew word behind this phrase can refer to a person's daily allotment of food. Either way it is read, the emphasis is on the zeal with which Job has sought to follow God.

**23:13-17** All the courage and confidence which Job has expressed in verses 4-12 is colored by the realization of God's absolute sovereignty. At this point, God's sovereignty is a threat to Job because he realizes that, despite the integrity of his case, there is no higher court of appeal to which he might turn should God not relent in his oppression of Job.

**23:13 he stands alone.** Literally, "God is one." Whether this echoes or anticipates Israel's confession that "The Lord our God, the Lord is one" (Dt 6:4) is uncertain, but its point is to stress God's unity of mind, will, and uniqueness. His will is the ultimate one that will be carried out in the world. **He does whatever he pleases.** Elsewhere, this truth served as a source of hope for Israel, in that it declared that no enemy could frustrate God's plan to save his people (Ps. 115:2-8). For Job, however, this truth was a threat (in that it implied that if God were determined to continue his plan of unjust suffering against Job, there was no person or force on earth or in heaven that could change the situation).

---

[1]Elizabeth Kübler-Ross, *On Death and Dying*, New York: MacMillan Publishing Co, 1969, p. 73.
[2]*The Grief Recovery Handbook*, New York: Harper & Row, 1988, pp. 22-23. This book contains many helpful suggestions on dealing with regrets over the past.
[3]*Don't Take My Grief Away*, p. 53.

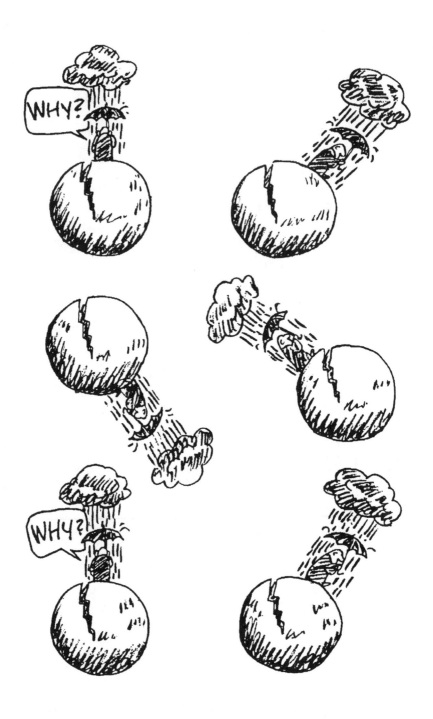

# Depression

**OBJECTIVE**

**The aims of the two sessions in this chapter are:**

- To consider the various ways in which depression is expressed during the grief process.
- To discuss ways to help ourselves and others deal with depression.
- To study a passage from Job in which his depression is expressed.

| 1 | Examining the Issue | 60 Minutes |

**OPEN**

**LEADER:**
Go around the group and, beginning with yourself, let each person respond *briefly* to the first question. Do the same for each question.

**"When the dog bites, when the bee stings, when I'm feeling sad..." (15 minutes).**

In *The Sound of Music,* Maria says that when these things happen to her she "simply remembers my favorite things, and then I don't feel so bad." Think back to when you were between six and ten years old:

1. What were some of your "favorite things"?

   - ❏ Christmas
   - ❏ the playground
   - ❏ stuffed animals
   - ❏ books
   - ❏ swimming
   - ❏ family vacations
   - ❏ your pet
   - ❏ a certain aunt (uncle)
   - ❏ playing games
   - ❏ other:_____

2. What made you feel sad when you were that age?

   - ❏ Being picked on by an older brother or sister
   - ❏ Having to wear a sweater when Mom thought I was cold
   - ❏ Not being allowed to watch television
   - ❏ Having to go to school
   - ❏ Being disciplined by my parents
   - ❏ Arguments with friends
   - ❏ Not being picked for the team
   - ❏ Having to wear glasses
   - ❏ Getting picked on by the school bully
   - ❏ Something else: _____

3. When you felt discouraged, what helped you get back on your feet?

- ❏ remembering my favorite things
- ❏ reading a good mystery
- ❏ doing something fun
- ❏ throwing a tantrum
- ❏ eating a snack
- ❏ talking to a friend
- ❏ talking to my Mom
- ❏ other: _____

4. When you feel discouraged now as an adult, what is one of your "favorite things" that helps you feel better?

**CONSIDER**

**Consider the following information about the role of depression in the grief process (5 minutes).**

**LEADER:**
Present this material while the group follows along in the text.

Depression marks the breakdown of our defenses in times of grief. The reality of our loss sinks in deeply. It surrounds us; it dominates us; it crushes us. As Granger Westberg, a pioneer in the interrelationship of religion and medicine, notes:

> Eventually there comes a feeling of utter depression and isolation. It is as if God is no longer in His heaven, as if God does not care. It is during these days we are sure that no one else has ever grieved as we are grieving.[1]

A woman who is dying becomes depressed when she realizes how many things she didn't accomplish in her life. She eventually comes to grips with this fact, deals with it, and dies in peace. Her husband, however (even years later) feels a sense of colorlessness and sadness whenever he visits places they used to go together.

According to Dr. Kübler-Ross, depression takes on different forms. In some cases, as for example when a person comes to grips with the fact that he or she is terminally ill, that person experiences what is called *preparatory depression.* He or she is faced with a situation in which nothing can be done to reverse the course of events. He or she will die. Period. Kübler-Ross writes:

> The patient should not be encouraged to look at the sunny side of things, as this would mean he should not contemplate his impending death.... The patient is in the process of losing everything and everybody he loves. If he is allowed to express his sorrow he will find a final acceptance much easier, and he will be grateful to those who can sit with him during this stage of depression without constantly telling him not to be sad.... In the preparatory grief there is no or little need for words. It is much more a feeling that can be mutually expressed and is often done better with a touch of the hand, a stroking of the hair, or just a silent sitting together.[2]

The second form of depression is *reactive depression.* This is the depression that sets in as a response to a major loss, such as a divorce, the death of a spouse, the discovery of a chronic illness (that will forever alter one's way of life), or the loss of a job. Besides feeling the pain of the immediate loss, the person can be overwhelmed with the changes and problems that accompany the loss. For example, a middle-aged woman whose husband dies suddenly faces not only the crushing pain of his death, but economic loss, possible relocation to a less expensive home, the pressures of an increased workload, complete child-care responsibilities, and a myriad of details relating to his death which need attention. The cumulative effect of all this can be quite debilitating.

There is no "normal" time frame for depression. The sense of loss ebbs and flows over time. Furthermore, depression may reoccur when memories are rekindled by a song, a sight, etc. Several years after his wife's death, one man became depressed at an auto show when he saw a 1937 Ford like the one he and his wife owned when they were first married. The grief process is like a spiral that keeps coming back to the same feelings with varying degrees of intensity and for various lengths of time.

These feelings cannot be mitigated by urging the person to "cheer up." To deal with depression, one must be reconciled with the past. This includes developing a self-identity that is not rooted in what has been lost. For the Christian, such stability can be found in one's relationship with Christ. Knowing that we are loved by God, knowing that this world is, indeed, passing away and that real glory is awaiting us, and knowing that God will never leave us nor forsake us (Jos 1:5) makes it possible to deal with our depression.

However, there is no such thing as automatically "getting over" a loss. No one can determine how quickly or how slowly a person will move through depression. Nor should pressure be applied to "get on with life." There are, however, some ways we can help others in their depression by:

- Helping them in practical ways, such as shopping for them, taking care of the children, and answering the phone.
- Being available to talk when they feel like doing so, but not insisting on conversation. Offering just to sit with them or to be involved with them in some quiet activity gives them the freedom to share without pressuring them to do so. Sending cards of support can communicate the same openness and care.
- Inviting them to be involved in activities with you. Even though they may not feel like talking, they may appreciate going to a store, visiting the ocean, raking leaves in the yard. Doing simple, ordinary things with those who care

for them is a genuine help for people in the midst of
depression.
- Praying for them and with them (as appropriate).
- Helping them see options they might consider as they
struggle to get back on their feet. This is not to make the
decisions for them or to push them into decisions. However, depression often blurs a person's ability to see the
choices available. We can help clarify alternatives so that
they can begin to act and make some choices again.

If you are the one who is depressed, the same principles apply:
- Let others into your life. You need them. Let them help you
with practical tasks. If you choose, you can ask them
simply to be with you and not talk much. That is okay. Just
don't cut yourself off from others.
- Keep a journal (as C.S. Lewis did).
- Meditate on God's promises.
- Don't allow yourself to sink into inactivity. Get involved in
some form of service to others, develop a new hobby, etc.
- Don't try to short-circuit depression in harmful ways, such
as through alcohol abuse, overworking, promiscuity,
overeating, etc.
- Face the fact of your loss squarely in all of its pain. Move
your sight from the loss to the future.

This is easier said than done, of course. The process of acceptance will be discussed in more detail in the next chapter.

**DISCUSS**

**Discuss with the group your response to the following
questions (15 minutes).**

1. What is it like when you feel depressed?
   - ☐ a slate gray afternoon
   - ☐ a cold, drizzling rain
   - ☐ a hot, oppressively humid day
   - ☐ a freezing morning with a bitter wind
   - ☐ a dull, overcast sky
   - ☐ a season of ankle-deep mud and slush

2. Can you identify with C.S. Lewis' description of grief as a
dog-tired man choosing to lie shivering rather than getting
up to find an extra blanket? Describe a time of depression
when you felt like this.

3. Although depression feels terrible, in what ways can it be
seen as a sign of progress in working through grief?

**RESPOND**

**Split into groups of four and discuss the following questions (25 minutes).**

1. Right now, what type of weather forecast best describes where you are in the spiral process of dealing with your loss?

   ❒ stormy conditions
   ❒ partly cloudy
   ❒ heavy rain
   ❒ a thaw
   ❒ chilly days
   ❒ sunny days ahead
   ❒ gentle Spring breezes are blowing

2. What would life be like if you chose not to work through depression when it came?

3. What was the most helpful thing anyone did for you during a time of depression? What was the most helpful thing you did for a friend who was depressed?

**LEADER:**
Ask each person, one at a time, to sit in silence. Go around the circle and allow the other three to share one positive quality they have seen in that person in the midst of the grief he or she has experienced. Do this for each member of the sub-group. End with a few moments in silence, or with short sentence prayers expressing thanks for the gift of one another.

4. Take a moment and think of one special quality that you have appreciated in each of the other three people in your group. You will have a chance to share this in a moment.

| 2 | **Bible Study** | 60 Minutes |

**OPEN**

**Sharing our Stories (15 minutes).**

During this time ask one or two members of the group to share in some detail his or her story of loss. No response is required from the group, except to listen attentively. Conclude the sharing by spending a few moments in prayer as a group.

**CONSIDER**

**LEADER:**
Present this material while the group follows along in the text.

**Read this introduction before you study the passage.**

Not surprisingly, Job went through periods of depression in the course of his grief. In the passage we are going to study, Job's sorrow is especially prominent as he reflects on the tremendous forces that seem to be aligned against him. Perhaps worst of all is the silence of God in the midst of his pain. A sense of abandonment, disappointment, betrayal, anxiety, and physical sickness all mark Job's depression. God, of course, is not absent or cruel or unjust—as Job will eventually discover. It just feels like this at the moment for Job. Depression is not a time of clear thought and accurate perception. It is a time of darkness and confusion. In this passage we confront head-on the many facets of depression.

**READ**

**LEADER:**
Allow group members time on their own to read the text and reference notes.

Read the passage below. Use the reference notes that follow to enhance your understanding of the text (5 minutes).

> [15] *"Terrors overwhelm me;*
> *my dignity is driven away as by the wind,*
> *my safety vanishes like a cloud.*

> [16] *"And now my life ebbs away;*
> *days of suffering grip me.*
> [17] *Night pierces my bones;*
> *my gnawing pains never rest.*
> [18] *In his great power [God] becomes like clothing to me;*
> *he binds me like the neck of my garment.*
> [19] *He throws me into the mud,*
> *and I am reduced to dust and ashes.*

> [20] *"I cry out to you, O God, but you do not answer;*
> *I stand up, but you merely look at me.*
> [21] *You turn on me ruthlessly;*
> *with the might of your hand you attack me.*
> [22] *You snatch me up and drive me before the wind;*
> *you toss me about in the storm.*
> [23] *I know you will bring me down to death,*
> *to the place appointed for all the living.*

> [24] *"Surely no one lays a hand on a broken man*
> *when he cries for help in his distress.*

*²⁵Have I not wept for those in trouble?*
 *Has not my soul grieved for the poor?*
*²⁶Yet when I hoped for good, evil came;*
 *when I looked for light, then came darkness.*
*²⁷The churning inside me never stops;*
 *days of suffering confront me.*
*²⁸I go about blackened, but not by the sun;*
 *I stand up in the assembly and cry for help.*
*²⁹I have become a brother of jackals,*
 *a companion of owls.*
*³⁰My skin grows black and peels;*
 *my body burns with fever.*
*³¹My harp is tuned to mourning,*
 *and my flute to the sound of wailing."*

         *Job 30:15-31*

**DISCUSS** | Discuss the passage with your group using the questions which follow (20 minutes).

1. What feelings does Job express in this passage? What are some of the causes of these feelings?

2. If you were doing a religious survey for the Gallup Organization at this moment in history and came upon Job, how do you think he would answer the following questions:

   - Job, do you believe in God?
   - Job, what are three adjectives that come to mind when you think of God?
   - Job, what is your major reason for believing in God?

3. Reviewing the passage as a whole, how would you describe Job's emotional, spiritual, and physical situation at this time?

4. Although depression feels terrible, in what ways might it be seen as a sign of Job's progress, in terms of abandoning the stages of denial, anger, and bargaining?

**RESPOND** | Wrap up your discussion with these questions (20 minutes).

1. With your current grief process in mind, place yourself somewhere on the scale and explain your response to the group.

| Not been depressed | Beginning to feel down | In the middle of heavy depression | I'm through most of my depression |
|---|---|---|---|

**2.** When you are depressed, with which of Job's feelings in this passage can you identify?

☐ terrified      ☐ overwhelmed
☐ fearful      ☐ in pain
☐ restless in the night      ☐ crushed
☐ afraid of death      ☐ afraid of God
☐ worthless      ☐ distressed
☐ churning inside      ☐ without peace

**3.** Which description of depression comes closest to your own experience?

☐ It is like an alien force that descends on me.
☐ Life feels wiped clean of meaning.
☐ Nothing seems to matter when I'm depressed.
☐ "The act of living is different all through" (Lewis).
☐ It feels like the depression will never go away.
☐ The feelings just come on their own and go away on their own.

**4.** What are some of the helpful ways you have discovered to deal with depression?

**5.** End with a time of prayer for one another.

**30:15-31** This is the conclusion of a section in which Job's past glory (ch. 29) is contrasted to his present humiliation (30:1-14). "This is perhaps the most pathetic of all Job's poems of grief.... It is more subdued, more reflective, less defiant. It shows Job in his weakness, no longer able to hope for even one touch of friendliness from men or God" (Andersen). In 30:1-11, Job expresses his anguish over the ridicule he received from people of low standing and in 30:12-15, he agonizes over the way death pursues him. His real grief, however, comes from the sense that it is God who is the one crushing him relentlessly (vv.16-31).

**30:15 Terrors.** In 18:11,14, Bildad used this word to personify death. "What Bildad predicted would befall the wicked has now overtaken Job" (Habel).

**30:17 Night pierces my bones.** God, rather than "night," should probably be read as the subject of this sentence (see vv.18-19) so that it reads "By night God..." **pierces.** Literally, "digs at" or "claws." Job's nocturnal torments were described more fully in chapters 3-5.

**30:18** The Hebrew text of this verse is unclear, but the image appears to be that of a man being attacked and choked as his assailant strangles him with his own clothing.

**30:19 mud.** This word has a double meaning. It can refer to literal mud (Is 10:6),, or to the ingredients out of which God fashioned humanity (4:19). The author is using it in an ironic way to demonstrate Job's unmaking, in that he is being reduced to the very mud from which he was originally formed. **dust and ashes.** Worthless materials. Job's identity and personhood is stripped of all dignity and meaning. He feels of no more value than the dust and ashes with which he has covered himself as a sign of his despair.

**30:20-23** Job moves from complaint (30:1-19) to a prayer for justice.

**30:20 I cry out to you.** The Hebrew word here implies not so much a prayer for help but a plea for justice. In the same way that Job had brought justice to the poor and oppressed who "cried for help" (29:11-17), so he pleads with God to do the same and hear his own plea for justice. **I stand up**. This draws upon the imagery of a person appearing before a judge to plead a case. Job attempts to do so with God, but is met with silence and a blank stare.

**30:21 You turn on me ruthlessly.** Literally,"You have become the cruel one against me." "The Cruel One" is a term used elsewhere to describe an enemy (Jer 30:14) and the terrible power of the monster Leviathan (41:1). Far from acting as a judge compelled to insure justice, God appears to Job as a fierce, cruel enemy who is bent on destroying him.

**30:22-23** Job feels as if God is driving him along like a leaf blown about by a fierce wind. The end result is that Job will be driven to death. Any sense of significance in life is snuffed out by the fact that he will share the same fate as anyone else, righteous or not. **the place appointed for all the living**. A sarcastic way of referring to the grave, the common lot of all humanity.

**30:24-26** Job pleads with God to treat him in the same way that others who are suffering are treated. Job himself had always been compassionate and just in dealing with those who suffered (29:11-17), and he expected that God would reward him for his efforts (29:18-20). Instead, he is met with evil. God seems less concerned with justice than an ordinary person would be. **good/evil**. This is in the sense of "good and bad fortune" (Habel).

**30:27 The churning inside me never stops**. Literally, "my intestines are in constant turmoil." In much the same way that people today speak of their "heart" metaphorically, the Hebrews referred to the "intestines" as the emotional center of a person (Jer 4:19 where "heart" is literally "bowels"). Because of God's apparent cruelty and lack of interest in justice, Job feels constant turmoil and a lack of peace.

**30:28 I go about blackened**. The meaning of this phrase is uncertain. This "has been referred either to dark attire, the unkempt skin of the mourner, the dark color of sackcloth worn in mourning, or the black skin of a leper... The phrase ["not by the sun"] makes it clear that the body and not the attire is referred to...Job's face has become black... through illness and misery" (Gordis). See also verse 30.

**30:29 a brother to jackals, a companion of owls**. Some versions translate "owl" as "ostrich." These animals live in deserted places and make mournful, haunting sounds. Job's appeals for justice "are as futile as the wail of a jackal or the screech of an ostrich in the wilderness (v.29). Instead of...defending his innocence against the accusations of his adversary, Job is forced to join the local mourners (v.31). He may as well weep for the dead as summon God to court." (Habel).

[1]*Good Grief*, p. 29.
[2]*On Death and Dying*, p. 77.

# Acceptance

**OBJECTIVE**

The aims of the two sessions in this chapter are:

- To consider what the idea of acceptance means as part of the grief process.
- To share where each of us are in terms of coming to grips with God and ourselves in light of our experience of loss.
- To explore a passage from the end of the Book of Job in which Job finally comes to accept his situation.

| 1 | **Examining the Issue** | 60 Minutes |

**OPEN**

**LEADER:**
Give the group a few minutes to work on the chart below. Then begin sharing your responses. For each item go around the circle, beginning with yourself, and give each person the opportunity to respond.

**Self Inventory (15 minutes).**

Put an **✗** on each spectrum line below to indicate how you are feeling about these four areas of your life.

About myself, I'm feeling . . .

|_____|

kinda blah                                     pretty good

About my loss, I'm feeling . . .

|_____|

awful                                               okay

About life in general, I'm feeling . . .

|_____|

despairing                                      hopeful

About God, I'm feeling . . .

|_____|

very cold                                         very warm

**CONSIDER**

**LEADER:**
Present this material while the group follows along in the text.

**Consider the following information about what acceptance means (5 minutes).**

Acceptance does not mean that the pain is all gone. Acceptance does not mean that I like what has happened. Acceptance does mean that I have stopped fighting the inevitable, and, to the best of my ability, that I am trying to adapt to the new situation with grace and dignity.

Once again, C.S. Lewis expresses this stage of grief beautifully when he writes about the comments of observers who assume he is "getting over" the grief of his wife's death:

> Getting over it so soon? But the words are ambiguous. To say the patient is getting over it after an operation for ap-

pendicitis is one thing; after he's had his leg off it is quite another. After that operation either the wounded stump heals or the man dies. If it heals, the fierce, continuous pain will stop. Presently he'll get back his strength and be able to stump about on his wooden leg. He has 'got over it.' But he will probably have recurrent pains in the stump all his life, and perhaps pretty bad ones; and he will always be a one-legged man. There will be hardly any moments when he forgets it. Bathing, dressing, sitting down and getting up again, even lying in bed, will all be different. . . All sorts of pleasures and activities that he once took for granted will have to be simply written off. Duties too. At present I am learning to get about on crutches. Perhaps I shall presently be given a wooden leg. But I shall never be a [two-footed creature] again.[1]

This type of acceptance is not a simple resignation to the reality of the crisis. Rather, it is an increasing ability to embrace the new reality and move on with one's life. For a dying person, this is often a quiet stage when his or her need to be comforted is probably far less than that of the anxious family. "He wishes to to be left alone or at least not stirred up by news and problems of the outside world. Visitors are often not desired and if they come, the patient is no longer in a talkative mood. . . This is a time when the television is off. Our communications then become more nonverbal than verbal. The patient may just make a gesture of the hand to invite us to sit down for a while. He may just hold our hand and ask us to to sit in silence."[2]

For others, acceptance may mean the ability to talk honestly about the new situation and make appropriate adjustments. Mildred Tengbom tells the story of Orville Kelly, who at age 42, discovered he had terminal cancer. She writes:

> Kelly learned to accept each day as a day of life with which he had been blessed. But getting to this place didn't just happen. After the doctor told him that he had cancer, he and his wife, Wanda unconsciously began to erect walls between themselves. They couldn't talk about the fact that he was dying.
>
> Kelly wrote: "One sunny afternoon I was driving back from a chemotherapy treatment in Iowa City. Beautiful fields stretched out ahead of me. Just for a moment I forgot about the cancer that was eating away my life.
>
> "Then I looked over at my wife beside me. I can't describe her look of sorrow and despair. It suddenly struck me how everything was falling apart because of me.
>
> "I wasn't dead yet; I wasn't ready to die yet; I wasn't going to die yet. In fact, I felt pretty good that day. But I had been creating my own hell on earth.
>
> "So I turned to my wife and said, 'Wanda, let's talk about it.' We had never really discussed the fact that I was dying.

...We did. It wasn't easy, I will admit. But you know, that night I knew a joy, peace and release I hadn't known for months."

Kelly later wrote: "Don't be afraid to die; don't be afraid to live. Do what you want to do. Pay for your mistakes, then start over. And happiness? How can you find it again? Go into your child's or your grandchild's bedroom, look at her face as she sleeps, bend down and kiss it. Go have a conversation with a friend. Walk out in your yard, look at up at the stars and pray. Ask yourself what you want out of life from now on. Thank God for all you have. Then perhaps happiness, as you call it, may begin to find you."[3]

Ultimately, acceptance means the willingness to live even with the reality of our pain, holding on to God as the source of our comfort (and not on to the person or object we have lost). Quoting Tengbom again:

So as we turn to God for help and receive it, we shall find ourselves able to accept loss. We let the yoke of suffering slip over our shoulders and rest there, assured it was made just for us. We enroll in this new class of pain. Accept the discipline of sorrow. Learn little by little to rise with praise and worship on your lips in the sacrament of pain. As we do so, peace and rest will come. The color will return to the flowers, the melody to the song of the birds, the flavor to food, and a smile to our faces. And we will find ourselves actually wanting to reach out to others in love and compassion.[4]

**DISCUSS**

**Discuss with the group your response to the following questions (15 minutes).**

1. In the course of their grieving, C. S. Lewis and Orville Kelly came to the point of acceptance of their losses. What strikes you as being the hardest part of the acceptance process?

   ❒ Acceptance means that I stop fighting.
   ❒ Acceptance means that, like Lewis, I come to know that I am now a one-legged person.
   ❒ Acceptance means that I (we) have to "talk about it" fully, and that is very hard.
   ❒ Acceptance includes long-term pain.
   ❒ Acceptance means moving beyond both my fear of dying and my fear of living.
   ❒ Acceptance means owning tremendous loss and all the feelings connected with that.

**2.** Marilyn Heavilin, in reflecting upon the deaths of three of her children, writes:

Recently a bereaved parent asked me if I wished I could bring my children back into this world. Of course I would love to have them back; that's an easy decision. But then as I reflected on all I have learned and how I have changed since their deaths, I thought to myself, I would love to have them back of course, but I would never want to be the Marilyn Heavilin I was before they died. I didn't know what life was all about. [5]

In what ways can you identify with Marilyn's feelings?

**RESPOND** | **Split into groups of four and discuss the following questions (25 minutes).**

**1.** Margaret Clarkson distinguishes between resignation and acceptance:

- *Resignation* is negative and passive. It carries with it the seeds of self-pity and self-imposed martyrdom.
- *Acceptance* is learning to "take from God's hand absolutely anything He chooses to give us, looking up into his face with love and trust."[6]

Put an ✗ to show where you are in your grief:

|_____|
resignation                                                    acceptance

**2.** Explain your response:
- ☐ I'm slowly coming to the point of willingness to live with the pain.
- ☐ I can accept my loss intellectually, but not emotionally.
- ☐ I'm still back in an earlier stage of grief.
- ☐ I'm still blocking out a lot of the pain.
- ☐ I refuse to accept this loss.
- ☐ I feel stuck in the area of resignation.
- ☐ I feel like Lewis and am just learning to use crutches.
- ☐ I have begun to accept the discipline of sorrow.
- ☐ I'm not even on this scale yet.
- ☐ Other:_____.

3. Kelly's story ends with him instructing us to "Thank God for all you have." Tengbom concludes by saying: "So as we turn to God for help and receive it, we shall find ourselves able to accept loss." What role does having a spiritual center in your life play in coming to a place of acceptance?

   ☐ It means more and more to me each day.
   ☐ I can't seem to turn to God for help right now.
   ☐ I want to have faith and hope in God.
   ☐ I just don't understand anything about God.
   ☐ Acceptance has come out of my trust in God.
   ☐ I'm beginning to know some peace as a result of turning to God.
   ☐ Other:_____.

4. What is one thing you feel you have learned about God through this time of loss?

5. What are some of the ways you feel you are changing for the better because of the experience of grief with which you are dealing?

   ☐ I'm more sensitive to others now.
   ☐ I have a heightened ability to feel.
   ☐ I have a clearer focus as to what is really important.
   ☐ I have a new openness to the spiritual side of life.
   ☐ I have a better appreciation of those I love.
   ☐ I know God better.
   ☐ Other:_____.

6. In closing, take some time to thank God for one another, and for the glimpses of him you have caught while dealing with your grief.

| 2 | **Bible Study** | 60 Minutes |

**OPEN**

**Sharing our Stories (15 minutes).**

During this time ask one or two members of the group to share in some detail his or her story of loss. No response is required from the group, except to listen attentively. Conclude the sharing by spending a few moments in prayer as a group.

**CONSIDER**

**Read this introduction before you study the passage.**

**LEADER:**
Present this material while the group follows along in the text.

Job's questioning of God and his struggle with his counselors continued unabated, until all of them were stilled by an over-powering revelation of God (Job 38-41).

In the section that follows (which is filled with beautiful images and powerful statements), God asks Job a series of questions by which he contrasts Job's knowledge with his own knowledge.

The result of God's questions is that Job is awed by the realization of the immense contrast that exists between God's power and wisdom, and his own understanding. Job quiets down and accepts that his situation is under the control of a wise and just God whom he can trust.

Interestingly, Job's questions as to why all this had to happen to him are never answered. God does not explain Job's situation. However, God does declare that the answers which the three counselors gave Job are false.

It is like this for most of us as well. We never receive an explanation for our loss. Pain comes. Loss is a part of life. This is all we know. The point is, however, to learn to center our lives around God, even as these things invade us. In any case, we will not necessarily be comforted by knowing *why*, but we can find comfort in knowing *who* is with us in those times.

In the end, then, Job is comforted not by slick and persuasive answers which reveal the "why" of his situation; he is overcome by the majesty of God as he reveals himself to Job. It is not answers but the sheer presence of God himself which brings about the peace Job has longed for.

**READ**

**Read the passage below. Use the reference notes that follow to enhance your understanding of the text (5 minutes).**

**LEADER:**
Allow group members time on their own to read the text and reference notes.

*¹Then Job replied to the LORD:*

> *²"I know that you can do all things;*
> *no plan of yours can be thwarted.*
> *³[You asked,] 'Who is this that obscures my counsel*
> *without knowledge?'*

*Surely I spoke of things I did not understand,*
*things too wonderful for me to know.*

*⁴["You said,] 'Listen now, and I will speak;*
*I will question you,*
*and you shall answer me.'*
*⁵My ears had heard of you*
*but now my eyes have seen you.*
*⁶Therefore I despise myself*
*and repent in dust and ashes."*

⁷After the LORD had said these things to Job, he said to Eliphaz the Temanite, "I am angry with you and your two friends, because you have not spoken of me what is right, as my servant Job has. ⁸So now take seven bulls and seven rams and go to my servant Job and sacrifice a burnt offering for yourselves. My servant Job will pray for you, and I will accept his prayer and not deal with you according to your folly. You have not spoken of me what is right, as my servant Job has." ⁹So Eliphaz the Temanite, Bildad the Shuhite and Zophar the Naamathite did what the LORD told them; and the LORD accepted Job's prayer.

¹⁰After Job had prayed for his friends, the LORD made him prosperous again and gave him twice as much as he had before.¹¹All his brothers and sisters and everyone who had known him before came and ate with him in his house. They comforted and consoled him over all the trouble the LORD had brought upon him, and each one gave him a piece of silver and a gold ring. ¹²The LORD blessed the latter part of Job's life more than the first. He had fourteen thousand sheep, six thousand camels, a thousand yoke of oxen and a thousand donkeys.¹³And he also had seven sons and three daughters. ¹⁴The first daughter he named Jemimah, the second Keziah and the third Keren-happuch.¹⁵Nowhere in all the land were there found women as beautiful as Job's daughters, and their father granted them an inheritance along with their brothers.

¹⁶After this, Job lived a hundred and forty years; he saw his children and their children to the fourth generation. ¹⁷And so he died, old and full of years.

*Job 42*

**DISCUSS**

Discuss the passage with your group using the questions which follow (20 minutes).

1. What do Job's words (vv.2-6) show about the way he has changed from what we have read about him in earlier passages? Describe Job's feelings in these verses.

2. If Job were deemed "blameless and upright" before his time of suffering (1:1), in what ways has he become a changed person after it? What "wonderful things" (v.3) does he understand now that he didn't before?

3. What is the significance of the fact that Job (despite his complaints and tirades against God) was commended by God for speaking what was right (v.7), while his friends (who upheld the traditional theology of that day) were charged with sinning?

4. Although Job's fortunes were amply restored, he still needed comfort from others (v. 11). Why?

**RESPOND**

**Wrap up your discussion with these questions (20 minutes).**

1. Job questioned God and struggled with his counselors until all of them were overwhelmed with an overpowering revelation of God. In what way is Jesus Christ an overwhelming revelation of God? In what ways is Jesus' suffering (and dying for our sins) God's answer to us?

2. How does Job's experience of God differ from the way you experience God? Does God speak to you more often from the whirlwind, or from the words and works of Jesus? Explain.

3. Job's story closes with a happy ending, but that was not the case for every person in the Bible:

   • Jeremiah died as a prisoner in Egypt, dragged there by his own people.
   • John the Baptist and the apostle James were beheaded.
   • Habakkuk suffered in the Babylonian invasion like any other Jew of the time.
   • Paul was executed by Nero.

   In light of what you know about the experiences of each of these heroes of the faith, what does "acceptance" mean when things *don't* get better physically or materially?

4. What are some practical steps you might take to cultivate a relationship with God even in the midst of your grief? How might others be of help to you in this?

5. In closing, take some time to thank God for one another, and for the glimpses of him you have caught even while dealing with your grief.

**REFERENCE NOTES**

**42:1-17** In chapters 38-41, God speaks to Job. While God does not reply directly to Job's complaints, neither does he accuse Job of any secret sins (of the sort that his friends were so sure had caused Job's sufferings). Instead, God forces Job to lift his eyes beyond the horizon of his own pain and consider God's rule throughout the cosmos. God's creative power, the beauty of what he has made, and the intricacy with which creation operates are all realities which Job has neglected. God's questions do not seek to discredit Job, rather they help him see the breadth of creation. These questions point out the fact that there are realities about which Job–and all people–are ignorant. In 40:7-41:34, God addresses the question which Job has raised about whether he has been unjust. Job had wanted to deal with things in a strict cause-and-effect manner on a personal level, but God calls him to consider the issue in cosmic terms. God's power and justice is seen in his domination of "behemoth" and "leviathan," two symbolic animals that represent the forces of evil and chaos which threaten creation. The point is that since God is the one who is engaged in battle with such forces (and is ultimately the only one who can subdue them) Job is in no position to accuse him of injustice. In chapter 42, Job acknowledges God's integrity and ceases his complaint (vv.1-6). God then rebukes Eliphaz and the other friends, thus justifying Job (vv 7-9). He ends by restoring Job to a place a wealth and honor (vv.10-17).

**42:2-3** Job quotes God's question in 38:2 and responds with the humble recognition that his understanding had, indeed, been far too limited. This does not represent a cowed submission, as though God fulfilled Job's fear of being overpowered so that the justice of his case wouldn't matter (9:17-18). Rather, it represents new insight and wisdom on Job's part regarding his own place in God's creation. He can now see his pain in the light of vastness of God's creation, and in terms of God's cosmic encounter with evil. His pain (even if it should continue) no longer threatens to rob him of significance, because he sees that it is not a product of the irrational activity of an angry deity.

**42:4-6** Quoting God's words in 40:7, Job has no further reply to God. His encounter with God transcends the limited, narrow conception of God that led to Job's questioning and doubt. Having met the God of creation, power, and goodness, his questions about God's fairness melt away into irrelevance. **despise myself/repent**. Having finally met God–as he so fervently desired–Job realizes that he has no case against God at all. So he withdraws his complaint.

**42:7-9** In an ironic reversal, God affirms Job's integrity while accusing the very people who, for so long, had assumed they were in the right. He charges them with the sin of which they had accused Job! Their stubborn insistence on a traditional understanding of how God ought to work (despite the inadequacy of that position to account for the real-life situation confronting Job) placed them in a position of judgment before God! They are thus in danger of receiving the wrath they thought Job was experiencing. The ultimate vindication of Job lies in the fact that God calls upon him to pray for his friends that they might be forgiven.

**42:8 My servant Job.** Far from being accursed by God, Job is publicly affirmed as his servant. In this context, he stands in the place of a priest, mediating God's forgiveness to sinners.

**42:10-17** The book closes with a brief description of how God restored Job as an affirmation of his integrity. All his wealth (measured in terms of animals) was doubled, and he once again was given sons and daughters (another traditional measure of God's favor upon a person) His life span of one hundred and forty years is double the traditional idea that a man's life is seventy years (Ps 90:10). His great age and peaceful death give him a place alongside the patriarchs Noah and Abraham as a model of faith and godliness.

**42:15** Including daughters in the father's inheritance was unusual.

[1]C.S. Lewis, *A Grief Observed*, p. 43.
[2]Elizabeth Kubler-Ross, *On Death and Dying*, p. 100.
[3]Mildred Tengbom, *Grief For A Season*, pp. 137-138.
[4]*Ibid.*, p. 130.
[5]Marilyn W. Heavlin, *December's Song*, pp. 132-133.
[6]*Ibid.*, p. 127.

# Hope

**OBJECTIVE**

**The aims of the two sessions in this chapter are:**

- To consider the role hope plays in helping us move through grief.
- To plan the next step for us personally and as a group.
- To explore a passage from Romans that powerfully expresses the basis for our hope.

| 1 | ## Examining the Issue | 60 Minutes |

**OPEN**

**LEADER:**
Go around the group and, beginning with yourself, let each person respond *briefly* to the first question. Do the same for each question.

**Waiting Around (15 minutes).**

1. When you were a child, can you remember having to wait for something that you wanted desperately then and there? What did you have to wait for?
   - ❏ Christmas
   - ❏ your own pet
   - ❏ a visit to a special relative
   - ❏ a new toy
   - ❏ your Dad to come home from work
   - ❏ a picnic lunch
   - ❏ summer vacation
   - ❏ your birthday
   - ❏ other:_____

2. What did it feel like to wait? How did you handle it?
   - ❏ not very well
   - ❏ I asked about it every few minutes
   - ❏ I tried to find something else to do while I waited
   - ❏ I threw a fit
   - ❏ I daydreamed about how nice it would be when it happened
   - ❏ other:_____

3. As an adult, when is it hard for you to wait?
   - ❏ in a checkout line at the supermarket
   - ❏ for my children to grow out of diapers (or get through adolescence)
   - ❏ for my boss to recognize my worth to the company
   - ❏ for God to clear up some of the puzzling questions I have
   - ❏ in traffic          ❏ other:_____

4. When you are in one of these "waiting" situations, what do you do to keep yourself from getting impatient?
   - ❏ I plan my day's work in my mind.  ❏ I talk.
   - ❏ nothing...I get impatient!          ❏ I pray.
   - ❏ I count to 10...or 1000.          ❏ I read a book.
   - ❏ I think about other things.          ❏ I get tense.
   - ❏ I reflect on how stupid the          ❏ other:_____
     person making me wait must be.

**CONSIDER**

**LEADER:**
**Present this material while the group follows along in the text.**

**Consider the following information about hope (5 minutes).**

Just as suffering is a universal human experience, so is the presence of hope in the midst of hard times. It is hope that sustains us when all else is bleak.

It is important, however, to distinguish between wishful thinking and hope. The two are not the same. Wishful thinking is a usually a form of denial ("It's not really so bad") or bargaining ("If I just pray hard enough, she won't die"). Wishful thinking is a delusion that a person chooses to embrace in an attempt to avoid the impact of pain. Wishful thinking ultimately disappoints because it does not deal with reality.

Hope, in contrast, is realistic. It does not allow a person to ignore the situation, nor to pretend that he or she has the power to stave off the inevitable by means of good intentions or will-power. Instead, hope allows the person to see beyond the pain, beyond the loss, beyond the hurt, to a deeper reality that provides a broader perspective in which to interpret the pain and loss of the moment.

What is that deeper reality? In a word, heaven. From the perspective of heaven and eternal life, human mortality loses its power to overwhelm us. Hope occurs when we brings heaven's promises into the here-and-now. Hope can trust in God's goodness in the midst of his hiddenness, because of the promise that we will one day see face to face what we only darkly perceive at present. Hope sees the truth of the future through the eyes of faith, and interprets the present in its light.

Hope differs from wishful thinking in significant ways:

• If wishful thinking is like a spark that kindles a flame which is, in turn, quickly extinguished by the next dose of reality, hope is like a steady warmth that gently but persistently radiates heat in any of the stages of grief.

• Wishful thinking is based on the way I think life should be. Hope is based on the way life really is. Hope is rooted in a thoughtful reflection on God's perspective of life and reality.

• Wishful thinking is a solitary delusion. While others see the facts for what they are, the individual caught by wishful thinking holds on to a fantasy. Hope is a shared experience, uniting a community through times of suffering.

• Wishful thinking has no place for suffering or loss. Hope honestly faces these experiences, interpreting them in the light of a bigger reality.

- Wishful thinking creates a sense of euphoria that is followed by an emotional crash. Hope is a persistent, steady source of growing emotional stability in the face of loss.

Kübler-Ross notes, "The one [coping mechanism] that usually persists through all [the stages of grief] is hope."[1]

In a chapter of a 1974 publication entitled *Grief*, the editors of The Christian Medical Society Journal wrote:

"Watch for Falling Rocks." Those words warn motorists navigating mountain highways in the western United States, but the signs seem wasted effort. If heavy boulders rumble down the mountainside, the traveler, no matter how careful, could not escape them. Any precaution against falling rocks must be taken before they fall.

What can be done to guard against the full impact of grief before it tumbles in on us? First, we can become aware of the way grief works. By understanding what happens at the time of bereavement, that it will happen, why our feelings and actions take the form they do, we will be less likely to be shocked, or terrified, or rendered helpless by the crush of emotion.

We can, in addition, guard carefully the relationships of life today. Regret is a child of grief, and looking back we often feel remorse for harsh words spoken, for kindnesses left undone, for opportunities to express and show love neglected....

We must also be certain about the center of our lives... the strongest grief comes when the core of life has been shattered...*Possessions* may so possess people that everything —family, church, occupation, recreation, friendships—is governed by that center. Then a depression wipes out savings and investments, and life crumbles in. *Power...* sometimes forms the hub of life. Then an election lost or the promotion fails to comes, and grief destroys because life's center is shattered.

*People*, too, can become a center. A family may provide the only reason for living, and existence may derive its color and strength from mate or offspring. Wives, husbands, children make good "spokes" but weak "hubs" [to life]. When a partner dies or children go off on their own, overwhelming grief may smother the person who remains.

Grief is lessened when we have an eternal center for our lives. The good news of the Bible is simply this: men and women may have a relationship with the eternal God through faith in Jesus Christ... Jesus Christ himself may become the hub of our entire life... In that relationship with God ... can be found a hub that no experience in life can destroy. [2]

**DISCUSS** | **Discuss with the group your response to the following questions (15 minutes).**

1. Reflect on people you have known who have gone through grief experiences. How does wishful thinking end up causing even more pain?

2. What difference does a belief in heaven make to a grieving person? Can you think of any promises of God concerning heavenly life which can comfort us in times of loss? Why isn't a belief in heaven wishful thinking?

3. Edgar Jackson concludes his book on grief with the story of Abraham C., the senior janitor of a large New York City apartment house and a deacon at a black Baptist church. When Abraham was taken to the hospital with a terminal illness, the pastor of a nearby church visited him regularly. The doctor told this pastor that Abraham had about a week to live.

   So the pastor started to talk to Abraham C. about the meaning of the spiritual values and the undying quality of the spiritual life. After an effort in that direction the patient looked up and said, "Pastor, you are being kind to me but you don't need to tell me all these things. The doctor hasn't told me yet but I know I will die in a few days. I am thankful for all of the good things the Lord has done for me all of my life. I have never wanted for anything that I rightfully should have had. I love the Lord and I know he loves me. I am not afraid to meet him face to face. He has been so good to me for so long, I know he will keep on being the same way. My wife and my friends have all gone on before me. Now I can go. So, pastor, don't you worry about me. I'm only going home and no one is unhappy about going home."[3]

In what ways does Abraham C. illustrate the place of faith and hope in a time of grief?

**RESPOND** | **Split into groups of four and discuss the following questions (25 minutes).**

1. There is no timetable for how fast people should move through the stages of grief. In reality, the stages are more like a spiral than a linear progression: a grieving person in the midst of one feeling begins to experience another, but then can be swept back around to the first feeling again. Given that reality, where do you see yourself at this moment in your experience of grief and loss:

   ❏ **Denial:** I still have a hard time believing this has really happened to me.
   ❏ **Anger:** I'm angry about things. I'm angry at God, myself, others. My anger is confused and unfocused a lot of the time.
   ❏ **Bargaining:** I think I'm negotiating with God and life. I keep playing the "if only..." game.
   ❏ **Depression:** I feel like giving up.
   ❏ **Acceptance:** I feel like I've come to terms with my loss, and am starting to get on with my life.

2. What is the basis on which your hope grows? Choose as many categories as apply to you:

   ❏ facing reality head-on and knowing I can make it
   ❏ knowing that God loves me and is with me
   ❏ the sustaining experience of being part of a caring community
   ❏ the inner experience of the warmth of hope
   ❏ seeing my loss in the context of the larger reality of God and his plan for the universe
   ❏ other:_____

3. How has your experience with grief and loss made you aware of the basis on which your life is built? What is one thing you have found helpful in strengthening the spiritual center of your life?

4. Conclude by praying together and committing one another to the care of God.

| 2 | **Bible Study** | 60 Minutes |

**OPEN**

**Sharing our Stories (15 minutes).**

During this final time of sharing, allow all those who have not yet told their stories to do so if they choose. If everyone has had the opportunity to share, discuss what sharing and hearing each other's stories has meant to you.

**CONSIDER**

**Read this introduction before you study the passage.**

**LEADER:**
**Present this material while the group follows along in the text.**

Christians are not immune to grief. Jesus himself is prophetically referred to as a "man of sorrows, and familiar with suffering" (Isa 53:3). The sufferings and losses that are the common lot of humanity do not bypass the person who trusts in Jesus. In some cases, that very commitment brings on suffering as other people ignore, reject, or ridicule the person who seriously considers the implications of following Jesus.

The early Christians in Rome experienced persecution because of their commitment to Christ. Paul knew this when he wrote the letter to the Romans. His encouragement to these Roman Christians, however, applies equally well to all people who suffer, regardless of the reason. The reason for this is that Paul views suffering not as an isolated experience, but as part of the whole fabric of creation. He understands that:

- Suffering is part of what all creation must in some way experience because of the presence of sin in the world,
- Ultimately, suffering is overruled by God's purposes for the good of his people,
- One day, there will be no more suffering; instead there will be full redemption, and
- Even now, suffering can be an opportunity to experience God's love.

**READ**

**Read the passage below. Use the reference notes that follow to enhance your understanding of the text (5 minutes).**

**LEADER:**
**Allow group members time on their own to read the text and reference notes.**

[18]*I consider that our present sufferings are not worth comparing with the glory that will be revealed in us.* [19]*The creation waits in eager expectation for the sons of God to be revealed.* [20]*For the creation was subjected to frustration, not by its own choice, but by the will of the one who subjected it, in hope* [21]*that the creation itself will be liberated from its bondage to decay and brought into the glorious freedom of the children of God.*

[22]*We know that the whole creation has been groaning as in the pains of childbirth right up to the present time.* [23]*Not only so, but we ourselves, who have the firstfruits of the Spirit, groan inwardly as we*

*wait eagerly for our adoption as sons, the redemption of our bodies.*
*²⁴For in this hope we were saved. But hope that is seen is no hope at all.*
*Who hopes for what he already has? ²⁵But if we hope for what we do*
*not yet have, we wait for it patiently....*

*³¹What, then, shall we say in response to this? If God is for us, who*
*can be against us? ³²He who did not spare his own Son, but gave him*
*up for us all—how will he not also, along with him, graciously give us*
*all things? ³³Who will bring any charge against those whom God has*
*chosen? It is God who justifies. ³⁴Who is he that condemns? Christ Jesus,*
*who died—more than that, who was raised to life—is at the right hand*
*of God and is also interceding for us. ³⁵Who shall separate us from the*
*love of Christ? Shall trouble or hardship or persecution or famine or*
*nakedness or danger or sword? ³⁶As it is written:*

> *"For your sake we face death all day long;*
> *we are considered as sheep to be slaughtered."*

*³⁷No, in all these things we are more than conquerors through him who*
*loved us. ³⁸For I am convinced that neither death nor life, neither angels*
*nor demons, neither the present nor the future, nor any powers,*
*³⁹neither height nor depth, nor anything else in all creation, will be able*
*to separate us from the love of God that is in Christ Jesus our Lord.*

*Romans 8:18-25; 31-39*

**DISCUSS** | Discuss the passage with your group using the questions which follow (20 minutes).

1. From what you know about Paul's life (and about the struggles experienced by the early church), what type of suffering does Paul have in mind as he writes these words?

2. Suffering (v.18), frustration (v.20), decay (v.21), pain (v.22), trouble, hardship, persecution, etc. (v.35) are universal experiences in this life. This is reality. However, in the midst of all this, Paul identifies various grounds for hope. Identify the reason(s) for hope in each of the following verses:
   - Verse 18
   - Verse 21
   - Verse 23
   - Verses 31-32
   - Verses 38-39

3. Although Paul does not explain the *why* of suffering in this section, what attitudes might he have had when he himself experienced hardship or loss? (To get a sense of Paul's real-life struggles, read 2 Co 11:23-30.)

4. Some Christians teach that if a person has enough faith, he or she will not have to experience pain or grief in this life, because God will spare such a person from suffering. Given this passage, how do you think Paul would respond to such a view?

**RESPOND**

**Wrap up your discussion with these questions (20 minutes).**

1. What is the difference in your experience between hanging on to wishful thinking and placing your confidence in the reasons for hope that Paul offers in this passage? Have you found any of these reasons for hope especially helpful to you? How?

2. From your experience, what nurtures this type of hope during times of grief? What steps, which you took *before* the rocks started to fall, have helped you?

**LEADER:**
You may find that some want to continue meeting, while others feel this is a good place to stop. If there are several different views about the next step, you might want to give people the option of meeting in sub-groups so those of like mind can plan their next step.

3. Given the nature of grief, it is important to realize that being a part of this small group does not automatically heal us. For some, this group experience may have helped them to name the hurt they are feeling. For others, the important thing may have been the opportunity to talk about their grief. For still others, the small group may have been a place where they felt genuine support and love. Now that these sessions are drawing to a close, what is the next step for your group? Some options are:

   ❑ Study together a book on the topic of grief and loss. Excellent books are available (see the Resource section).

   ❑ Get some professional help in dealing with a situation that does not seem to be improving.

   ❑ Continue to meet as a group to work through the sections in this book that you had to skip over the first time (if you did the course in 7 weeks).

   ❑ Start one or more new grief support groups for others who would find such a support group helpful, led by members from this group (or by those with professional experience in this field).

   ❑ Get involved in a grief support group in your community. There may be one sponsored by your local hospital for specific types of grief work (such as with cancer patients, diabetics, heart patients, or death-related issues). Al-Anon can be of help to people dealing with the loss experienced as the result of an alcoholic spouse or child. Some communities have divorce recovery groups.

   ❑ Continue meeting as a group, but study a new topic. Call Serendipity at 800-525-9563 for suggestions and for a free catalog of other materials.

&#9633; Disband as a group, but have a reunion meal in a month to see how everyone is doing.

&#9633; Other _____.

**LEADER:**
Allow each group members time to express what he or she is grateful to the others for.

4. What have you learned from each other during these weeks together? Take a few minutes to identify new insights, attitudes, etc. that have been important to you. Share these with the others.

5. Close the meeting with sentence prayers of thanks for each person in the group, as well as prayers for the specific concerns each is dealing with.

## REFERENCE NOTES

**8:18 present sufferings.** Specifically, the persecutions Christians experience. These are real, not pleasant, but slight in comparison with the glory ahead.

**8:19-21** The fate of humanity and fate of the universe are intertwined. Just as through Adam's sin, creation fell, so through the redemption of the sons of Adam will creation itself be restored.

**8:20 The creation.** The whole of the non-human world, both living and inanimate. **was subjected.** The verb tense indicates a single past action. See Genesis 3:17-19. **frustration.** At the present moment, creation is unable to achieve the goal for which it was created (that of glorifying God), because the key actors in this drama—humanity—have fallen. **in hope.** There was divine judgment at the Fall, but this was not without hope.

**8:21 will be liberated.** Creation will be freed from its frustrating bondage when the children of God are also freed from the last vestiges of sin. **bondage to decay.** All of creation seems to be running down; deterioration and decomposition characterize the created order.

**8:22 pains of childbirth.** Such pain is very real, yet is temporary and is the prelude to new life. The image is not of the annihilation of the present universe, but of the emergence of a transformed order.

**8:23 we...groan inwardly.** One groans not just because of persecution, but because one is not yet fully redeemed. Believers' bodies are still subject to weakness, pain, and death. The believer therefore longs for the suffering to end and for the redemption of the body to be complete. **we wait eagerly.** In one sense, a Christian is already an adopted child of God; in another sense, he or she has yet to experience fully that inheritance.

**8:31-35** In one of his most eloquent passages, by means of five rhetorical questions, Paul asserts that absolutely nothing can separate Christians from God's love.

**8:33-34** Paul's next two questions are set in the context of a law court. Since God is the Judge (who has already justified them) and Jesus is their Advocate (who pleads for them), there is no charge that can bring about a Christian's condemnation.

[1]Elisabeth Kübler-Ross, *On Death and Dying*, pp. 122.
[2]*Christian Medical Society Journal*, Volume V, Number 4, 1974.
[3]*Understanding Grief*, New York: Abingdon Press, 1957, p. 236.

# Resources For Further Study

The *Serendipity Bible for Groups* contains a number of Questionnaire Bible Studies. There are two parts to each of these Bible studies. The first half (*Looking into the Scripture*) examines the text itself; the second half (*My Own Story*) reflects on the text in the context of our lives. Both parts use questions which are followed by a series of "answers" from which you are asked to choose. Generally there is no "right" answer to these questions. The "answers" reflect your understanding and your experience. The name for this sort of small group exercise is relational Bible study, since the focus is more on the people in the group than on delving deeply into the text. You can do more rigorous Bible study by using the questions in the margin of the *Serendipity Bible for Groups*.

Some of these Questionnaire Bible Studies can be adapted to enable you to do further study of the issue of grief and loss. What follows are fourteen suggested studies—seven from the Old Testament and seven from the New Testament. While these questionnaire studies do not always focus directly on grief and loss, they all discuss some aspect of the topic. You will need to adapt the studies so that they focus more closely on the issue. Brief suggestions are given below on how to focus the study. These studies are listed in the order in which they occur in the Bible, not in the order in which you will necessarily want to study them.

## Studies from the Old Testament

1. God's Grief Over Sin and Promise to Noah (Genesis 6:5-8; 8:13-22), page 45.
   Focus on how and why God grieves.

2. Abraham Tested with Issac (Genesis 22:1-19), page 65.
   Focus on the pain of both Abraham and Issac.

3. Joseph Sold by his Brothers (Genesis 37:12-36), page 89.
   Focus on the pain and loss felt by Joseph.

4. Nathan Rebukes David (2 Samuel 12:1-14), page 415.
   Focus on David's grief over his sin.

5. The Still, Small Voice (1 Kings 19:1-19), page 469.
   Focus on Elijah's depression.

6. Job Tested (Job 1:1-22), page 644.
   Focus on the nature of loss as seen in Job's experience.

7. Jonah Runs Away From God's Call (Jonah 1:1-17), page 1187.
   Focus on Jonah's anger and depression.

## Studies from the New Testament

1. The Christ Must Die (Matthew 16:13-28), page 1267.
   Focus on what it meant for Jesus to know that he soon would be facing rejection and death.

2. Death of Jesus (Matthew 27:45-56), page 1289.
   Focus on Jesus' experience of death.

3. Gethsemane (Mark 14:32-42), page 1320.
   Focus on Jesus' pain in the face of his approaching death.

4. Temptation of Jesus (Luke 4:1-13), page 1337.
   Focus on the difficult issues with which Jesus had to struggle.

5. Jesus Rejected at Nazareth (Luke 4:14-30), page 1338.
   Focus on the pain of rejection.

6. On the Road to Emmaus (Luke 24:13-35), page 1384.
   Focus on the joy found on the other side of death.

7. Raising of Lazarus (John 11:1-44), page 1413.
   Focus on the power of Jesus over death.

**FOR FURTHER READING**

Heavilin, Marilyn W., *December's Song,* San Bernadino CA: Here's Life Publishers, 1988.

Kübler-Ross, Elisabeth, *On Death and Dying,* New York: MacMillan Publishing Co, 1969.
   • This is Kübler-Ross' classic study of the process of grief.

Koop, C. Everett, *Sometimes Mountains Move.*
   • The story of the death of former Surgeon-General Koop's son in a mountaineering accident.

Jackson, Edgar N., *Understanding Grief,* New York: Abingdon Press, 1957.
   • One of first books written to help ministers understand the nature of grief and how to respond to it.

_____. *The Many Faces of Grief,* Nashville TN: Abingdon Press, 1977.

James, John W. and Cherry, Frank, *The Grief Recovery Handbook: A Step-by-Step Program for Moving Beyond Loss,* San Francisco: Harper & Row, 1988.
   • An excellent and well-tested step-by-step plan for recovery for those who are dealing with grief.

Lewis, C.S. *A Grief Observed,* New York: Seabury Press, 1961.
   • A deeply moving account by Lewis of the death of his wife Joy, characterized by burning honesty and profound faith.

Linn, Dennis & Linn, Matthew, *Healing Life's Hurts: Healing Memories Through the Five Stages of Forgiveness,* New York: Paulist Press, 1978.
   • The grief process from an inner healing point of view.

Manning, Doug, *Don't Take My Grief Away: What to Do When You Lose a Loved One,* San Francisco: Harper & Row, 1979.
   • A very practical book written by a minister for those who have just lost a loved one, with sections on arranging the funeral, dealing with grief, and living as a single person again.

_____. *Comforting Those Who Grieve: A Guide for Helping Others,* San Francisco: Harper & Row, 1985.
   • A briefer book which repeats many of the ideas in the first book, but with some new comments on running grief groups.

Raphael, Beverly, *The Anatomy of Bereavement,* New York: Basic Books, 1983.

Tengbom, Mildred, *Grief for a Season*, Minneapolis MN: Bethany House Publishers, 1989.

Westberg, Granger E., *Good Grief: A Constructive Approach to the Problem of Loss*, Philadelphia: Fortress Press, 1971.

Wolterstorff, Nicholas, *Lament for a Son*, Grand Rapids, MI: Wm. B. Eerdmans, 1987.
> • A poignant account of the death of his son in a mountaineering accident, written by an eminent Christian Reformed philosopher.

**FOR FURTHER HELP**

Many communities offer help and support for people facing crises. Some hospitals offer support groups for people (and their families) dealing with cancer or other life-threatening diseases. Counseling agencies–either privately run or state-sponsored–also offer grief groups for people dealing with death, divorce, injuries, and other severe losses.

The Compassionate Friends is a nationwide support system for people dealing with bereavement. They can be contacted at: Compassionate Friends National Headquarters, P.O. Box 1347, Oak Brook IL 60521.

John W. James and Frank Cherry (who wrote *The Grief Recovery Handbook*) run the Grief Recovery Institute (8306 Wilshire Blvd., #21-A, Los Angeles, CA 90211) which sponsors seminars on grief. Much of their work is geared to assisting those in the helping professions to learn how to help others deal with grief.